Studies
in
Philemon

Studies
in
Philemon

by
W. Graham Scroggie

KREGEL PUBLICATIONS
Grand Rapids, Michigan 49501

STUDIES IN PHILEMON
Published in 1977 by Kregel Publications, a
division of Kregel, Inc. All rights reserved.

Printed in the United States of America

Library of Congress Cataloging in Publication Data

Scroggie, William Graham, 1877-1958.
  Studies in Philemon.

  Reprint of the 1927 ed. published by Hulbert Pub. Co.,
London, under title: A note to a friend.
  1. Bible. N. T. Philemon — Commentaries. I. Title.
BS2765.3.S39   1977   227'.86'07   77-79186
ISBN 0-8254-3718-0

CONTENTS

INTRODUCTION

Superscription (1-2)

1. The Writers

2. The Readers

Benediction (3)

1. The Blessings

2. The Blessers

Verses 1-3

Paul, a prisoner of Christ Jesus, and Timothy our brother, to Philemon our beloved and fellowworker. And to Apphia our sister, and to Archippus our fellow-soldier, and to the church in thy house; Grace to you and peace from God our Father and the Lord Jesus Christ.

1

INTRODUCTION (1-3)

Philemon, III John, and possibly II John are the only strictly private letters of the Apostolic Writings which have been preserved.

The Letter to Philemon, which like the other two just referred to is little more than a note, has been admired by men whose views on the Scriptures were most divergent. Luther says, "this Epistle showeth a right noble lovely example of Christian love." Calvin, referring to Paul, says, "though he handleth a subject, which otherwise were low and mean, yet, after his manner, he is borne up aloft unto God." And Franke, "the single Epistle to Philemon very far surpasses all the wisdom of the world." Ewald pronounces it "surpassingly full and significant." Sabatier says, "we have here only a few familiar lines, but so full of grace, of salt, of serious and trustful affection, that this short epistle gleams like a pearl of the most exquisite purity in the rich treasure of the New Testament." Baur says, "it is penetrated with the noblest Christian spirit." And Holtzmann pronounces it to be "a pattern of tact, fine feeling, and graciousness."

Short as the letter is, yet no less than eleven persons are mentioned in it: five at the beginning — Paul, Timothy, Philemon, Apphia, Archippus; five at the end — Epaphras, Mark, Aristarchus, Demas, and Luke; and throughout, the central figure, the subject and occasion of the letter, is Onesimus.

The Apostle Paul wrote this note about 62 A.D., during

9

his first Roman imprisonment, and it was sent to Colossae by the hand of Onesimus at the same time that Tychicus conveyed the letter to the church in that town.

The object Paul had in view was the reinstatement in the service of Philemon of Onesimus his slave, who had robbed him and run away.

Onesimus had fled to Rome, and by a providence, the details of which are not given, he met Paul, who led him to Christ, and who now sent him back to his Christian master to be not merely a slave but "a brother beloved" (verse 16). We nowhere read of the effect of the Apostle's effort, but we are sure that it accomplished all that was expected.

SUPERSCRIPTION

1. THE WRITERS

Paul

What a story that name recalls! How richly endowed a personality! Paul, the preacher, the pastor, and the man of prayer; Paul, the chief of sinners, the Christian, the scholar and the saint; Paul, the theologian and controversialist, missionary and friend; Paul, the mystic and the statesman! Well may Sir William Ramsay speak of the "charm of Paul." Next to his Master he is the most discussed man in Christendom today. It was Paul, Jesus Christ's Apostle to the nations, the master-builder of the universal Church and of Christian theology, who wrote this little note to a friend on a purely domestic matter. Truly does Calvin say, "with such modest entreaty doth he humble himself on behalf of the lowest of men, that scarce anywhere else is the gentleness of his spirit portrayed more truly to the life."

"That must have been a great intellect," says Dr. Maclaren, "and closely conversant with the fountain of all light and beauty, which could shape the profound and far-reaching teachings of the Epistle to the Colossians, and pass from them to the graceful simplicity and sweet kindliness of this exquisite letter; as if Michelangelo had gone straight from smiting his magnificent Moses from the marble mass, to incise some delicate and tiny figure of love or friendship on a cameo."

In taking up his difficult task, notice how Paul speaks of himself: "a prisoner of Jesus Christ."

A Prisoner. He almost always speaks of himself as an apostle, but he has the wisdom to fit the designation to his object. In writing to the churches, the thing which he makes prominent is his *authority.* But that would not do here. He does not think it seemly to command Philemon what to do with Onesimus. He prefers to entreat (verses 8-9), and he can better entreat as a *prisoner* than as an apostle. He is making appeal to Philemon's *compassion* rather than to his *conscience,* and so with unartificial spontaneousness and unconscious pathos he opens with these words — "Paul, a prisoner. . . ."

This note he strikes three times again in this brief letter (verses 9, 10, 13) and so makes it practically impossible for Philemon to refuse his request.

Asking will often succeed where commanding will altogether fail.

Of Christ Jesus. Paul says, "I am a prisoner," not of Nero, nor of Rome, but "of Christ Jesus." It is a *captive* who is pleading for a *slave.* If Paul's speaking of himself as a "prisoner" reveals his *tact,* his relating his captivity to Christ Jesus reveals his *faith.* He shuts his eyes to all secondary causes and sees in his imprisonment, as Joseph long before had seen in his, an all-wise Providence.

Christ Himself had riveted his manacles on Paul's wrists; therefore, He bore them as lightly and proudly as a bride might wear the bracelet that her husband had clasped on her.

This simple word is the expression of a great truth. The events in the life of every Christian have both human and divine aspects, primary and secondary causes. I have mentioned Joseph. We know what part his brothers played and how altogether guilty they were; yet at last Joseph said to them, "As for you, ye meant evil against me; but *God meant it for good,* to bring to pass, as it is this day, to save much people alive" (Genesis 50: 20). So was it with Christ Himself. We know what share the Jews and the Romans had in the crucifixion; yet Christ says that He laid down His life of His own accord, and that God so loved the world that He gave Him to die for us. These are not contradictions but two aspects of one great truth. It is the lesson of Jeremiah 18: 3-4. The wheels represent the human aspect, and the hands, the Divine. Paul was "a prisoner of Christ Jesus." The Jews and the Romans must bear their share of guilt in His ever having been on the Cross, but how great would the Church's loss have been had he never been there! Not only would we have lost this pure gem of private correspondence, but the profound revelations of the Ephesian and Colossian Epistles, and also that intensely human document, the Epistle to the Philippians. Indeed, may we not say that we would have lost the whole Bible!

They must take the responsibility who persecuted Bunyan and Rutherford, but how vast had been our loss had they not thus suffered.

When Paul says that he is "a prisoner of Christ Jesus," he means that he is there according to the will of God and in consequence of loyalty to Christ.

He is Christ Jesus' prisoner, not Jesus Christ's. The latter name refers to Him on earth, the former to Him as risen and enthroned. Paul is the prisoner of Him whom he saw that day when he was smitten down on the Damascus road.

It would be well if we always saw the divine aspect of our afflictions, if our ruling consciousness was rather of the "hands" than of the "wheels." Such a view would temper our troubles, and we would be troubled less with our tempers.

Timothy

When Paul writes "and Timothy," his greatness shines out again, because, as a matter of fact, this letter is not from Timothy; it is Paul's from start to finish. Why, then, does he mention Timothy? Perhaps, because Philemon and his household were known to Timothy who was with Paul during a great part of his three years sojourn in Ephesus (Acts 19: 22). Perhaps, because of the fact that he was to be Paul's successor, and this association of names would secure for the younger man a measure of recognition. And also, no doubt, because of Timothy's keen interest in the case of Onesimus.

Paul was always generous of recognition and was especially the friend of young men.

Notice how he introduces Timothy. He is "the brother." The designation is simple and eloquent, as is "the sister" of the next verse. It tells not only of relationship but also of friendliness and loyalty. Paul might well have spoken of Timothy as his son, for he was his spiritual father. But he chooses a relationship which is wider: he was a "brother," not only to Paul, but to Philemon, and to all Christians.

2. THE READERS

To Philemon

All that we know of this man is contained within this Epistle and one or two sentences in the Colossian letter. From these references the following facts emerge:

(1) Philemon was a Gentile; (2) he was a Colossian (Colossians 4:9; Philippians 2); (3) he was married and had a son; (4) he was led to Christ by Paul (verse 19), probably during the Apostle's long residence at Ephesus; (5) he was characterized by evangelical zeal, as the meeting of believers in his house indicates; (6) he was large-hearted and generously disposed, as is reflected by his hospitality (verses 5 and 7); (7) he was well-to-do, a fact made evident by the two previous circumstances and by the added fact that he owned one slave, and perhaps more.

Observe how Paul addresses Philemon, calling him "our dearly beloved."

Our beloved. The test of discipleship, which the Lord set, was the mutual love of those who believe in Him (John 13:34; 15:12 and 17). Paul here recognizes this toward Philemon, and he will in a moment or two ask Philemon to recognize it towards Onesimus (verse 16). The Apostle, writing as he does for the reinstatement of a slave who is now a Christian, puts love in the forefront. No motive less strong than Christian love could move Philemon to take such a course. Paul begins, therefore, by telling Philemon that he is loved by all the brethren. But, further, he speaks of Timothy as "our fellow worker."

Our fellow worker: Paul mentions others as fellow workers at the end of the letter (verse 24). The reference is, in all probability, twofold. It reminds Philemon of the time, during Paul's three years stay at Ephesus, when he helped the Apostle in the work of the gospel. In what ways he helped we do not know; but that he would do so is certain.

But the reference is more than reflective. It is designed to assure Philemon that he is still a fellow worker with the apostles and all true Christians. For Christians to be fellow workers, they need not be on the same ground; neither need they live in the same generation. We who are laboring for Christ today are fellow workers with all who have gone before us from the beginning.

Diversity of work, variety of temperament and gifts, widely separated fields, and different periods of time do not impair unity of service. What better illustration can we have than the one before us.

He who reaps is fellow worker with him who ploughed and sowed. The first man who dug a shovelful of earth for the foundation of Cologne Cathedral and he who fixed the last stone on the topmost spire a thousand years later are fellow workers.

Philemon and Paul: the one lived a Christian life and helped some humble saints in an insignificant, remote corner; the other flamed through the whole then-civilized, western world, and sheds light today; but the obscure, twinkling taper and the blazing torch were kindled at the same source, shone with the same light, and were parts of one great whole.

Let us therefore correct our standards of judgment. Let us adjust our perspective that we may truly see the importance of all service rendered to Christ by the best-known and the least-known. We may then draw inspiration from the fact that, having all the same Master, we are all fellow workers and all share in the final reward.

To Apphia

That Apphia was mentioned at all, and at this point in the letter, has a significance much beyond what one would at first think. We assume that she was the wife of Philemon. It is evident that she, too, was a Christian (sister, or beloved); she also was wronged when her husband was wronged by Onesimus, so that it was necessary that she, too, should be disposed to give the returning slave a friendly reception. The way in which she is addressed implies that she and her husband were like-minded and whole-hearted in the work of hospitality and in housing a church. How much of the practical part of such service devolves upon the Christian matron we all know, and how impossible it all would be without her sympathetic cooperation we also know. So this letter is sent to her also. But there is a further significance in the mention of Apphia. The old world was parted by gulfs deep and wide, the chief being the distinctions of race, condition, and sex. But as the Christian Gospel was destined to do away with all such distinctions, Paul exclaims:

"There is neither Jew nor Greek" — race.

"There is neither bond nor free" — condition.

"There is neither male nor female" — sex.

The degraded classes of the Greek world were slaves and women. This epistle touches both and shows us Christianity in the very act of elevating both. So Paul sets the wife by the side of her husband, yoked in all exercise of noble end.

The divinity of the Gospel is nowhere more manifest than in its attitude towards women, and children, and the poor. Apphia is designated as are all the others.

Two readings are possible, Beloved (Authorized Version) or Sister (Revised Version). Lightfoot says that "the preponderance of ancient authority is very decidedly in favor" of the latter.

Christian men and women are brothers and sisters, having a common origin and Home, a common life and common obligations. These expressions, *brother* and *sister,* are not to be bandied about until they become part of the phrase stock of cant, but what they signify should become evident in true Christian life and love. Let every Christian man remember that every Christian woman is his *sister;* let every Christian woman remember that every Christian man is her *brother,* not in word but in deed and in truth. A nobler and purer atmosphere will pervade the Christian Church, making life sweeter and stronger.

To Archippus

It has been thought that Archippus was the spiritual leader of the church that met at Philemon's house, but it is practically certain that he is mentioned here, because he was the son of Philemon and Apphia. We have, therefore, a beautiful picture of a Christian household in that Phrygian valley: father, mother and son.

That Archippus did discharge some special ministry, probably in the Church of Laodicea, is clear from the reference to him in the Colossian letter (4: 17). Laodicea was within walking distance of Colossae, and the son would be in constant touch with his parents; it is, therefore, most natural that he should be mentioned in this letter, because Paul would secure for Onesimus the fullest welcome.

Philemon is a "fellow worker"; Apphia is a "sister"; and Archippus is a "fellow soldier."

If fellow worker tells of *achievement,* fellow soldier speaks rather of *endurance;* and every Christian is called to both (Philippians 2: 25).

But why is Archippus called here a fellow soldier in preference to any other designation? Maybe the explanation will be found in Colossians 4:17, where a gentle warning is given to Archippus to fulfil his ministry. It would seem that he was in danger of becoming slack; perhaps his zeal was cooling. We know that this was the sin of the Laodicean Church (Revelation 3), and if Archippus was the pastor of it at this time, the warning is the more significant.

In writing to Philemon, Paul has nothing of this in view, or, if it were in the Apostle's mind, he approaches it from the opposite standpoint, by encouraging instead of warning this young man. He is not only a Christian soldier, but a fellow soldier with this greatest of soldiers.

The tact of the Apostle is consummate, and it is set before us not only to be admired but also to be emulated. There is need in most cases not only for rebuke but also for encouragement; and, further, there are right times and ways of administering them.

We would have supposed that the rebuke would have been given in this private note, and the encouragement in the public letter (Colossians). But, presumably, that would not have been as effective; moreover, it would have introduced a jarring note into the harmonies of this little epistle.

Let us ever seek to do the right thing, in the right way, at the right time, from the right motive, and then what we do will certainly be right.

To The Church in Thy House

Obviously, what is meant by these words, "to the church in thy house," is that a company of believers met for worship in Philemon's house. Other cases of such gatherings are known; for example, Romans 16:5; I

Corinthians 16:19. Lightfoot tells us that "there is no clear example of a separate building set apart for Christian worship within the limits of the Roman Empire before the third century, though apartments in private houses might be specially devoted to this purpose."

If there were many Christians in Colossae they could not all meet in one house. In all likelihood they were divided into little groups which met in stated places, one of these being Philemon's house. The letter is addressed to this group of Christians as well as to the family, because, if Onesimus is received back by Philemon, he would be a member of this Christian circle. It was important, therefore, to secure their good will.

The Apostle had overlooked nothing which was calculated to give effect to his request. I have no doubt that, first and last, he would make the whole thing a matter of prayer (verses 4, 6), but in addition, he did all he could toward answering his own prayers.

How beautiful an example of a Christian household: husband, wife, and son rejoicing together in the grace of Christ and finding their friendships and fellowships among those of like mind. What a rebuke this picture is to many a so-called Christian household.

Philemon's was not a "house divided against itself"; it has therefore stood while much, which at that time seemed to be of far greater importance, has passed away.

Is there a church in your house? Is your household a church?

BENEDICTION

1. The Blessings

Grace

Grace is one of the greatest words in the Christian vocabulary. We are not likely to explore all its meaning, to sound all its depths, nor to scale its illusive heights. Yet we must not leave it in the abstract, or we shall miss what may be known of its meaning. This may be said to be threefold.

Grace stands for the whole sum of the unmerited blessings which come to men through Jesus Christ. It means the unconditioned, undeserved, spontaneous, eternal, stooping, pardoning love of God, and thus it describes a disposition in the Divine nature. It then comes to mean the manifestation and activities of that disposition, the Divine love in exercise. Finally, it points to all the fruitful results in the believer's life of those Divine operations.

From this we see how singularly full is the meaning of *grace* — with its *fountain* in God, its *flow* from God to us, and its *fulness* in ourselves. Of His fulness we all receive grace for grace, wave upon wave as the ripples press shoreward, pulsation after pulsation of unbroken light.

It is this that Paul wished for Philemon and his household at Colossae, and what more or better could he wish? Yet, this is not all. He wrote, "Grace to you, and peace. . . ."

Peace

Peace is another essentially Christian word, and so it was sung by the angel chorus that announced the advent of the Savior. It presupposes a need; it implies war, strife within and among us; and it assures us that this need not be. The content of *peace,* as of *grace,* is threefold: peace with *God,* peace with *ourselves,* and peace with our *fellows.*

We first have *peace with God;* then, the *peace of God;* and finally and ever more we realize that ours is the *God of peace.* Where this peace is, spiritual and social harmony is restored, and the raging passions of the soul are stilled. It secures also a true adjustment of relations. That is why Paul introduces it here. The harmony in this house has been broken, and the relations have become disordered. It is urgently necessary that peace should again sit upon the throne, that peace which is expressive of a right relationship between God and man. It will be well now to look at these blessings together.

Grace and Peace.

Here the Western and Eastern forms of salutation blend. *Grace* is Greek, and *peace* is Hebrew. In combination the force of each is strengthened. Their relation to one another is vital.

"Grace to you and peace" is the usual Pauline greeting, but nowhere is the order inverted. It is always "grace and peace." These stand related to one another as root to fruit, as spring to stream, as cause to effect, as center to circumference, as foundation to superstructure.

The peace of God never precedes the grace of God; there must be the expression of grace on His part before there can be the experience of peace on our part. In all the manifold forms in which restless hearts need peace, the peace of God brings it to them.

Sometimes *mercy* is added to *grace* and *peace.* It then becomes the link between grace in God's heart and peace in ours.

Paul is quite sure that if grace reaches Philemon as it might and should do, peace also will come to his heart and home.

The benediction is both a prayer and a prophecy. Paul asks for these blessings for the Colossian family, and he is confident that they will have them. But Paul is not content to wish his friends these blessings; he would lead their thoughts and affections to the blessers.

2. THE BLESSERS

Just because these blessings of grace, mercy, and peace have their origin in God are they available for us. But there is here much more than that inspiring thought. The blessings are "from God our Father and (the) Lord Jesus Christ."

At least three great truths are to be found here.

God Our Father

From Him are grace and peace; He is their *fontal source.* Paul grounds the appeal he is here making, not on our creational relationship to God, but on a relation by redemption. It is "God our *Father.*" On that ground alone could He show us grace and give us peace, and on that ground, consequently, should Philemon exhibit grace and establish peace relative to the subject of this letter. "God," Paul would say, "is your Father, yours Philemon, and mine, and Onesimus' too"; and unless that is recognized all around, we cannot know as we should either the grace or peace of our Father. And then he adds, "the Lord Jesus Christ".

Lord Jesus Christ

In writing to a father, Paul reminds him of the Father. But Philemon is also a master, and so the Apostle reminds him of the Master of us all.

Paul gives Him His full title. We see Him *human* in Jesus, *divine* in Lord, *official* in Christ.

The Christ was the meeting place of God and man in one Personality. God comes to us through the Lord, Christ Jesus; and we draw near to Him through Jesus Christ, the Lord.

If the Father is the fontal source of grace and peace, the Son is the flowing stream. These blessings could not come to us from either of the Divine Persons alone.

But there is a further thought here that must not be overlooked. In 2 John 3, we read, "Grace, mercy, and peace, *from* God (the) Father and *from* (the) Lord Jesus Christ, the Son of the Father."

Father and Son are One

But in our passage there is only one preposition governing both names, *"From* God our Father and (the) Lord Jesus Christ."* The first passage emphasizes the distinction between Father and Son, but our passage emphasizes their unity.

That the name of Christ is associated in this way with that of God the Father is an undesigned recognition, as it is a plain revelation of the Deity of Christ. Only God can give "grace and peace"; He, therefore, Who gives these is God.

The prepositions in the two above passages are not the same, being παρα in John, and ἀπο in Philemon. In so far as there is any difference of meaning in this connection, the former (παρα) signifies that these blessings are *in* and *with* God before they are *from* Him; while the latter (ἀπο) points rather to the fact that they are really communicated to us, coming "away from" Him.

We may now stand back from this minute analysis of Paul's introduction, see on how broad and strong a foundation his appeal is made to rest, see by how ample a revelation he would move Philemon to Christian action, and see how profound are those truths in the light of which we Christians are to order our conduct down to its smallest details.

He is about to ask a Christian master to receive back into his service a slave who had robbed him and run away, but who since has been converted to God. How will the apostle Paul approach the subject?

By a full and generous recognition of relationships human and divine.

Paul himself is Christ Jesus' prisoner. Timothy is a Christian brother. Philemon is beloved, and a fellow laborer. Apphia is a Christian sister. Archippus is a fellow soldier. The household is a Christian Church. God is the Father of them all. Jesus Christ is the Lord of them all. The divine grace is available for them all. The divine peace may be possessed by them all. Paul prays that it may be so; and he is confident that it will be so.

All this is only the first of three distinct stages of approach to the request he intends to make, and it reveals in what noble setting Paul saw all the events and details of the Christian life. Every time, he "hitched his wagon to a star." It reveals also the kindliness and courtesy, too rare among Christians, which yet counts for so much in the complex life and exacting service of today.

When a servant of God with a world reputation such as Paul had, associates with his name a much younger Christian and calls him brother, he, by that act, wins a devoted friend and disciple.

When a field-marshal, such as Paul was, speaks of a private, such as Archippus was, as a fellow soldier, he may reckon on that Tommy to follow him in the fight to the death.

When a master workman, such as Paul was, speaks of an obscure person like Philemon as his fellow worker, he has made him capable of better work than ever before.

It is this milk of human kindness that feeds our hearts; it is generous acknowledgment and praise, such as Paul bestowed, that tone up life and service, and make men and women capable of unthought-of deeds.

Let us from this simple yet profound introduction learn what Christianity is at its best.

COMMENDATION

Paul's Prayers for Philemon (4-7)

Thanksgiving (4-5, 7)

1. The Cause

2. The Motive

Supplication (4-6)

1. The Occasion

2. The Purport

Verses 4-7

I thank my God always, making mention of thee in my prayers, hearing of thy love, and of the faith which thou hast toward the Lord Jesus, and toward all the saints; that the fellowship of thy faith may become effectual, in the knowledge of every good thing which is in you, unto Christ. For I had much joy and comfort in thy love, because the hearts of the saints have been refreshed through thee, brother.

2

COMMENDATION

Paul's Prayers for Philemon (4-7)

Bishop Lightfoot's paraphrase of this section is:

> I never cease to give thanks to my God for thy well-
> doing, and thou art ever mentioned in my prayers. For
> they tell me of thy love and faith; thy faith which thou
> hast in the Lord Jesus, and thy love which thou
> showest towards all the saints.
> And it is my prayer that this active sympathy and
> charity, thus springing from thy faith, may abound
> more and more, as thou attainest to the perfect
> knowledge of every good thing bestowed upon us by
> God, looking unto, and striving after Christ.
> For indeed it gave me great joy and comfort to hear
> of thy loving-kindness and to learn how the hearts of
> God's people had been cheered and refreshed by thy
> help, my dear brother.

This pregnant section is in two parts, but these are so
run into one another that only with care are they discerned and disentangled. One part is *praise,* and the other is
prayer; but the Apostle's heart is so full that his words
have no time to form logical sequence. We must, however,
for a right understanding of them, separate these parts.
The section will then read as follows:

Paul's Praise for Philemon's Love

"I thank my God always . . . hearing of thy love . . . which thou hast toward the Lord Jesus. . . . For I had much joy and comfort in thy love, because the hearts of the saints have been refreshed through thee, brother."

Paul's Prayer for Philemon's Faith

"I make mention of thee in my prayers, hearing of . . . the faith which thou hast . . . toward all the saints; that the fellowship of thy faith may become effectual, in the knowledge of every good thing which is in you (us), unto Christ."

These two parts taken together follow the structure known as inverted parallelism,

> a) love (5)
> b) faith (5)
> b) faith (6)
> a) love (7)

Let us now examine these words in detail.

PAUL'S THANKSGIVING

"I thank my God." That is the note on which Paul generally begins (the letter to the Galatians and the second to Corinth are the exceptions) and on which we also should begin, unless we can give good reason for doing otherwise. There is usually much in the character and conduct of our fellow Christians for which to give praise, and the exercise is good alike for those who give it and those who get it.

Christian praise is never fulsome flattery, and at its best it will always, as here, be given to God rather than to the individual, though in the individual's hearing and for his benefit.

Further, the giving of thanks should be a habit with us.

Paul says, "I thank my God *always.*" If it was not for one person or thing, it was for another. No life is so utterly barren of good as to present no ground whatever for thanksgiving.

1. THE CAUSE OF PAUL'S THANKSGIVING

The occasion of Paul's thanksgiving was a report which had reached him — "hearing," he says — and no doubt it was Epaphras who had brought the good news. But the cause of his thanksgiving was the thing reported, namely the *love* and *faith* of Philemon. Observe first of all:

The Structure of This Fifth Verse

The qualities are first mentioned — *love* and *faith,* and then the objects toward whom they are directed — *Christ* and the *saints.* We have already seen that the structure of the whole paragraph is an inverted parallelism. This verse follows the same arrangement:
   a) thy love,
      b) and the faith which thou hast,
      b) toward the Lord Jesus; and
   a) toward all the saints.
From this it will be seen that the *love* is toward the *saints,* and the *faith* is towards the *Lord;* and that the latter is placed between the two parts of the former, between the quality, *love,* and the objects of it, the *saints.*

Maclaren has likened this arrangement to "the pathetic measure of *In Memoriam.*" Thus we have, as it were, "faith towards the Lord Jesus" imbedded in the center of the verse, while "thy love . . . toward all the saints," which flows from it, wraps it round.

The Qualities for Which Thanks are Given

Together with hope, we speak of love and faith as the Christian graces, the superlative virtues. Elsewhere the Apostle says, "And now abideth faith, hope, love, these three." They are classed together under the government of a verb in the singular, showing how intimately, and vitally they are related. Hope is not mentioned in our passage because it was not germain to the purpose which the Apostle had in view.

Further, with reference to that purpose, it should be noticed that the Apostle departs from the usual order, and places *love* before *faith*. It is a delicate touch, spontaneous and artless, arising out of, and calculated to secure the object he had in view in writing this note, namely, to call forth to new activity the love of Philemon. What Paul wanted his friend to do was not so much a *work of faith*, as a *work of love;* and so he mentions love first.

Nor must we overlook the relation to one another of these qualities. *Love* the *stream* is first named, and then, *faith* its *source*. The *circumference* is first shown, and then, its *center*. The *effect* is here made to enfold the *cause*.

Love and faith should never be separated, though they may be, as we learn from 1 Corinthians 13. Where there is love there is sure to be faith, but, alas, there may be faith in the absence of love. Faith is a foundation, and love a superstructure, and while the superstructure presupposes the foundation, it is possible to have the latter without the former.

It was possible of Philemon to be strong in faith and weak in love, and it is his love that Paul now appeals to, though in speaking of it he reminds him of the rock on which it rests.

The Objects Toward Which These Qualities Move

Faith is toward the *Lord Jesus; Love* is toward all *the saints.* We have seen that faith and its object are imbedded in love and its objects: thoughts 2 and 3 are set between 1 and 4, and as faith toward God precedes love towards man, we ought to consider the former first.

Faith toward the Lord Jesus. The New Testament teaches that Christ is alone the true and worthy object of the faith which is trust.

We nowhere read of "faith toward all the saints"; that would be asking too much. Complete reliance can be placed in One alone. But this passage is specific. It says, "Faith toward the Lord Jesus."

In these names, *Lord* and *Jesus, Christ's* divinity and humanity blend. He whom we trust is both God and Man. As God alone, we could never have known Him. As Man alone, He could never have saved us. But as the God-Man, He is revealed as Redeemer. He expects our trust and is worthy of it.

Another thought in this great utterance is not so obvious, the thought suggested by the preposition *toward* (προς). Maclaren's paragraph on this must be quoted in full:

The idea is that of a movement of yearning after an unattained good. And that is one part of the true office of faith. There is in it an element of aspiration, as of the soaring eagle to the sun, or the climbing tendrils to the summit of the supporting stem.

In Christ there is always something beyond, which discloses itself the more clearly, the fuller our present possession of Him is. Faith builds upon and rests in the Christ possessed and experienced, and therefore will it, if it be true, yearn towards the Christ unpossessed. A great reach of flashing glory beyond opens on us, as we round each new headland in the unending voyage.

Faith is toward the Lord Jesus, reaching out after Him, and ever more fully finding Him. This *faith* is the *root* of which *love* is the *fruit*. Now we turn to the enveloping clause.

Love toward all the saints. In Galatians 5:6 Paul speaks of "faith working through love." Ideally, *faith* is the inspiration of *love,* and *love* is the manifestation of *faith.* A *loveless faith* is cruel, and a *faithless love* is sentimental. The true relation of these qualities to one another should never be forgotten. Observe who are the objects of love, "the saints."

One point of the compass, faith, is fixed in the center, Christ Jesus; and the other point, love, describes the great circumference which embraces all the saints.

Of course, love is also toward the Lord Jesus. We cannot truly love one another aright, if we do not first love Him. Paul here relates the love to the saints, probably for two reasons: first, because where there is love toward the saints, love toward God is assumed; second, because he was writing to draw out Philemon's love towards a saint.

And this brings to notice another point, namely, that Christian love is to be toward *all* the saints. Philemon's love is to be active, not only towards Paul, but also towards Onesimus. It is much easier to love some people than others, but it is a Christian duty to love all. Well may we pray, "Lord increase our love!"

It will help us if we remember that the love referred to is not the love of natural affection, but the love of divine principle. It is not the love which awaits to be drawn out by its object, but is the very love of God, shed abroad in our hearts, and ever active towards the least worthy.

Lightfoot points out the change of prepositions here, from πρὸς to εἰς. Faith is, "πρὸς τον κυριον Ιησουν"; but love is, " εἰς παντας τους ἁγιους." He says, πρὸς signifies direction, and εἰς, arrival and so *contact*. Faith aspires *toward* Christ; and love is exerted *upon* men.

2. THE MOTIVE OF PAUL'S THANKSGIVING (7)

Plainly, Paul's motive was gratitude. Verse 7 connects with the beginning of verse 4, "I thank my God . . . for I had much joy and comfort."

This paragraph begins and ends on the note of praise, praise for the love of Philemon.

His love was practical, for it met needs and made impressions. Through him the hearts of the saints had often been refreshed, and not by words only, but by deeds. The detailed record is not on earth, but in Heaven. It is not by one great sacrifice on our part that the hearts of others are made stout for the journey and strong for the task, but by the constant performance of the petty kindnesses, no one of which might be worth recording, but which, in the aggregate, constitute a sublime record.

Paul would say, "As you have done, brother, so continue to do, and do for him who hands you this letter, Onesimus." The thanks which Paul had given to God for Philemon's past good deeds would encourage him to do one more, and one that, no doubt, would tax his capacity to love; that is, to receive back, as a brother, a robber-slave. Yet, what Philemon had done led Paul to believe that he would do this also; so he praises for what is past, and trusts for what is to come.

Another thought is here, namely, that good deeds done in one place may be powerfully felt in another; that what is done in one age may be graciously fruitful in succeeding ages. When Philemon refreshed the hearts of these Colossian saints, he little thought that his action would give joy and comfort to Paul his friend, far away in a Roman prison.

A small pebble cast into a lake will start circles which, ever-widening, will reach its banks, however far apart. In like manner the smallest deeds and words, good or bad, have an expanding influence. What is done or said here may be carried by the winds like seeds to the ends of the earth, to make or mar, to gladden or sadden other souls.

PAUL'S SUPPLICATION

We have seen that Paul's praise was more especially for Philemon's love; now we are to see that his prayer is more for Philemon's faith.

1. THE OCCASION OF THE PRAYER (4-5)

The same report that led Paul to praise sent him to prayer. These two can never lie far apart, for where there is occasion for the one, there is almost certainly need for the other. In the letter to the Philippians there is the same conjunction. Paul does not in this, or directly in the next paragraph, say how he would have Philemon's love to act. He will tell him in a moment or two. But he does here and now say how he would have Philemon's faith to act.

2. THE PURPORT OF THE PRAYER (6)

We shall only barely state the significance of this brief but pregnant prayer. There are three clauses. It is, as to its *matter*, that Philemon's fellowship — active sympathy and charity, springing from his faith — "may become effective," that is, may abound more and more.

As to the *means,* it is that he may go on to attain to the perfect knowledge of every good thing in him. And finally, this activity of faith is to have for its *motive* and end the glory of Christ.

From this we learn that Christian fellowship can flow only from Christian faith; such fellowship is always practical; because of its origin and nature, it is effective; the exercise of such faith springs from knowledge and leads to knowledge; conduct, the product of character, in its turn produces character; and that the goal and final resting-place of all our good purposes and performances is Christ Himself.

Thus, on the way to make request for Onesimus, Paul tells Philemon of his praise and prayer on his behalf; and so prepares the way for Philemon's acquiescence.

APPROACHING THE OBJECT OF THE LETTER

Paul Might Enjoin (8)

1. His Right

2. His Reason

Paul Only Entreats (9)

1. The Ruling Principle

2. The Personal Plea

Verses 8-9

Wherefore, though I have all boldness in Christ to enjoin thee that which is befitting, yet for love's sake I rather beseech, being such an one as Paul the aged, and now a prisoner also of Christ Jesus.

3

APPROACHING THE OBJECT OF THE
LETTER (8-9)

The first word in this paragraph, "wherefore," connects what follows with the preceding verse and paragraph (verse 4-7). It is as though Paul is saying, "I have heard of your love, and now to your love I appeal. You have by its exercise refreshed the hearts of the saints; and I am confident that you will continue so to do; making their need, and not your personal feeling, your ground of action."

All this time the Apostle has Onesimus in mind, and is preparing Philemon for the mention of his name, and the request he is about to make. This ingenuity and tact to secure the reception of the runaway slave are a recognition of how unpleasant some duties are, even to the best of God's people, and of the necessity of our being urged to these duties in the way best calculated to get them performed.

All Christian duties are not pleasant, and any worthy means which can render the performance of them less distasteful should be adopted.

The Apostle, who knew the hearts of others so well, because he so well understood his own, uses this argument: "You have done good; there is good to be done. Your past kindnesses constitute a reasonable ground of expectation that you will not be unkind even to the most unworthy." That is the force of the "wherefore."

In these two verses Paul is still approaching the matter which occasioned the letter, and it is instructive to notice how he does so. He here intimates that he is about to make a request, but he does not yet say plainly what it is. What he does now say is, "I might enjoin, but I prefer to entreat. Did I enjoin, I would be well within my right and would have good reason for so doing, but I entreat on the strength of the highest principle of action supported by a personal plea."

Let us look then at these details and draw from them something of their abiding teaching.

PAUL MIGHT ENJOIN (8)

Paul declares that he might enjoin both in *right* and *reason*.

1. HIS RIGHT TO ENJOIN

"I have all boldness in Christ to enjoin thee."

By *boldness* he means *freedom*; he is at liberty to command Philemon with reference to Onesimus. This right attaches to his apostolic authority, a note which is struck early in most of his epistles. He was commissioned and commanded of God to commission and command, and this prerogative of the Apostle's was recognized.

This right does not belong to the Christian minister today as it did to the apostles. Their commission was special and limited to the life-period of that circle.

But even with them the right was not without limit and safeguard. Paul recognizes this when he says "in Christ." His freedom, liberty, boldness was in Christ. By Christ he had been called; for Christ he had been set apart; and only in Christ did he exercise his ministry.

These two words reveal both the scope and the limit of Paul's authority. If in Christ he had a right to command, then how commanding was that right.

If again his right was only in Christ, how careful he must be not to presume upon it in the energy of the flesh.

So in our manifold relations, carrying with them, as they do, certain rights, we should learn that the exercise of these rights is conditioned; that the relations in which we stand to one another should be regulated by our common or special relation to Christ; and that there are times, when, to insist on the exercise of our rights, would betray a want of tact, if not indeed moral weakness.

Let the present case serve as illustration. Had Paul used his apostolic authority and commanded Philemon to take back Onesimus, in all probability he would have failed of his object; or, had he succeeded, as to the outward fact, he certainly would not have done so as to the inward spirit.

To waive one's rights is, more often than not, a sign of strength and grace. To his right to enjoin, Paul adds:

2. His Reason in Truth

"That which is befitting."

Here again, his "boldness" or liberty has both its scope and its limit appointed.

As to *limit:* Paul had no right in reason to command anything that was not becoming. Not even apostolic authority could commend such a course to any enlightened person. But, on the other hand, as to *scope:* the reason that such a course as Paul had in mind was "befitting" would greatly support his apostolic right.

The word he here uses, translated "that which is befitting," occurs only twice again in the New Testament and both are in the prison epistles (Ephesians 5:4; Colossians 3:18). In all three instances the word has the force of what is, or is not *becoming* as to moral obligation. When Paul says it is *befitting* that Philemon receive back Onesimus, he means a great deal more than that it is eminently desirable that he should do so. He means that, as a Christian, Philemon is under moral obligation so to do, and that if he declines, he will be chargeable with a flagrant neglect of his duty.

It was the strength of Paul's request that enabled him so readily to lay aside his authority and make appeal to Philemon on the merits of the case. It is as though he is saying, "There is no need for me to bring to bear my apostolic authority; the duty is so obvious, and your sense of obligation is so true, that the matter has but to be put before you, and, distasteful as it may be to the flesh, much as it may go against your grain, you will do your duty."

Can we be trusted in this way? Have we this fine sense of what is morally becoming?

Paul, then, could command, but he will not. It is not always well for us to do all that we can do. There is a power in power restrained, in right reserved. There are good and better ways of accomplishing desirable ends, and we should always choose the better.

This leads us to the second part of our paragraph.

PAUL ONLY ENTREATS (9)

"I have all boldness to enjoin . . . yet . . . I rather beseech."

We must all feel, as Philemon did, that his request is much more powerful than his command could have been, that his call is more compelling than any charge.

1. The Ruling Principle of His Entreaty

"For love's sake."

It would seem that the reference is not to Philemon's love for Paul, or Paul's for Philemon, but to love as a Christian principle of action, at all times and everywhere. The Apostle had just been commending Philemon's love and thanking God for it. He will not now command it, but appeal to it, confident that nothing more is necessary.

Love must ever remain the greatest motive to noblest action, just because it carries with it the heart as well as the reason. Love does not stop to nicely calculate the strict requirements of duty, but acts spontaneously and generously. Maclaren says, "Authority is the weapon of a weak man, who is doubtful of his own power to get himself obeyed, or of a selfish one, who seeks for mechanical submission rather than for the fealty of willing hearts. Love is the weapon of a strong man who can cast aside the trappings of superiority, and is never loftier than when he descends, nor more absolute than when he abjures authority, and appeals with love to love."

Loyalty to duty may save our Christian countenance in the eyes of the world, but only wholehearted love to Christ will make the Christian life attractive to men.

It is to such love that Christ appeals. He does not say, "If ye keep my commandments, ye will love me" but, "If ye love me, keep my commandments." It is not duty that inspires us to love, but love that moves us to duty. Paul understands the heart too well to mistake the note he should now strike.

A true man will do his duty. A true Christian will do more. The one will be moved by a sense of obligation; the other, by the divine impulse of love.

It is love that gets things done when everything else

fails.

2. The Personal Plea in this Entreaty

"Being such an one as Paul the aged, and now a prisoner also of Christ Jesus."

It will be a sorry day when sentiment counts for little or nothing in our choice of action. Sentiment is not sentimentality. Sentiment is emotion awakened by things that appear to have worth.

It is to sentiment that Paul now appeals, and his appeal is legitimate.

He has said, "Philemon, I am about to ask of you something which I have a right to command. It is something eminently becoming, and I appeal, not to your sense of duty, but to your Christian love." He now adds, "In considering my request, will you please remember that I am an old man and am in prison far from home."

This last touch is an illustration of consummate artlessness. The power of it is at once felt. It is an appeal to sentiment as far from sentimentality as anything could well be.

Paul's first plea is on the count of his *old age.* He was not old, if years be reckoned, being only about sixty, but he was worn by work and suffering. At any time the end might come. His life was behind him, and his reward just before.

But what had that to do with Philemon receiving back Onesimus? Paul puts it into the scale as something that should weigh with his friend. It is as though he said, "Not much longer shall I be here to make requests of you; not much longer will you have opportunity to give me joy and comfort. I am old and tired."

The appeal on the ground of old age is one that might

not be so effective today, when, alas, regard and respect for the aged are not shown as once they were. With Philemon, at any rate, it would count. There is an alternative reading which substitutes *ambassador* for *aged,* and though this is supported by Lightfoot, it is not followed by the revisers, except in the margin; the substitution impresses one as being out of harmony with the spirit and purpose of this appeal.

Paul's second plea is that he is a *prisoner*: a prisoner also. It is sad enough to be in prison for the best of causes when one is young, but it is a great trial when one is old.

Of course, Paul was not at this time in a cell, but in his own hired house, and at liberty to receive his friends (Acts 28). Yet it was captivity, and everyone loves his freedom. Philemon was free, but Paul was not; and the elder man puts in that plea.

Yet, he does not groan about his condition; rather, he glories in it, for he says that he is "a prisoner of Christ Jesus." This is how he began his letter, and he returns to it more than once. The Jews and the Romans must take the responsibility for his being there; yet, behind all human hatred, is the divine hand. Paul was in prison at Rome within the plan of God.

This plea, therefore, is not only pathetic, but also majestic; it is not only tender, but also heroic; and it would go a long way to secure Paul's object.

Then, do not let us despise personal and secondary motives in order to reinforce duty which is binding from other and higher considerations. If Paul can get his friend to do the right thing by the help of these subsidiary motives, still, it is the right thing; and the appeal to these motives will do Philemon no harm, and, if successful, will do both him and Onesimus a great deal of good.

Now Paul is ready to mention the objectionable name. He has taken 133 words out of a total of 333 to get to the matter in hand. But this is not mere verbiage; every word counts. Elihu, in the *Great Drama,* takes 52 lines to say that he is going to speak. But he was a young man, and Paul was an old man; that perhaps accounts for it.

DISCLOSING THE PURPOSE OF THE LETTER

The Request (10-12)

    1. Father and Son

    2. Past and Present

    3. Sent to be Received

The Desire (13-14)

    1. I Would Have Kept, but . . .

    2. You Had Not Given

The Situation (15-17)

    1. The Way of Providence

    2. The Slave and Brother

    3. The Deputy Partner

The Promise (18-19)

    1. I Owe You

    2. You Owe Me

Verses 10-19

I beseech thee for my child, whom I have begotten in my bonds, Onesimus, who once was unprofitable to thee, but now is profitable to thee and to me: whom I have sent back to thee in his own person, that is my very heart: whom I would fain have kept with me, that in thy behalf he might minister unto me in the bonds of the gospel: but without thy mind I would do nothing; that thy goodness should not be as of necessity, but of free will. For perhaps he was therefore parted from thee for a season, that thou shouldest have him for ever; no longer as a servant, but more than a servant, a brother beloved, specially to me, but how much rather to thee, both in the flesh and in the Lord. If then thou countest me a partner, receive him as myself. But if he hath wronged thee at all, or oweth thee aught, put that to mine account; I Paul write it with mine own hand, I will repay it: that I say not unto thee that thou owest to me even thine own self besides.

4

DISCLOSING THE PURPOSE
OF THE LETTER (10-19)

Relative to the length of the letter, the Apostle has been a long time coming to the point he had in mind in writing it. But he has now reached it, and so he definitely asks Philemon to take Onesimus back.

The disclosure of the purpose of the letter, occupying verses 10-19, is in four parts as follows:

The Request (10-12)
The Desire (13-14)
The Situation (15-17)
The Promise (18-19)

These verses it will repay us to consider in detail, so full are they not only of "the milk of human kindness," but of principles far-reaching in their effects upon our lives and institutions.

THE REQUEST (10-12)

The most natural parts of this section are those furnished by these three verses, each of which throws into prominence one idea. The idea spoken of in verse ten is:

1. FATHER AND SON (10)

"I beseech thee for my child, whom I have begotten in my bonds — Onesimus."

Paul's Loving Solicitation for Onesimus

"I beseech thee for . . . Onesimus."

The extrordinary tactfulness which the Apostle has displayed thus far in the letter is here also in evidence. Indeed this is the critical sentence in his letter.

He now ventures to mention the offensive name, but everything may depend upon how he does it. The order of the words in the original text indicates his hesitation to write it supported by thought and tactfulness; and then, he puts it last, not first.

Perhaps nowhere is the Apostle more thoroughly Christian than here; and by *Christian* I mean *like Christ*. Had Onesimus been the most distinguished person of his day, or Paul's own son gone astray and needing to be pleaded for, the Apostle could not have exhibited more earnest and loving solicitation. But Onesimus was not distinguished, except for crime; and he was at the other end of the social scale from Paul, poor, ignorant, and hated; yet this man, whose name was to flame down nineteen hundred years, pours upon this slave his love, as the woman poured her ointment upon Jesus. That is a product only of the Christian faith.

The famous letter of Pliny to Sabinianus on behalf of an offending servant of the latter is curt and cold in comparison with Paul's to Philemon. The one is based throughout on a religious motive; the other, on a casual and somewhat contemptuous feeling of kindliness.

It is only as that love of Christ, which led Him to die for the lowest, is shed abroad in our hearts, that we shall think of and feel for the very least of His ransomed ones, as Paul did for Onesimus. This is one of the glories of Christianity, and something which the world cannot imitate or counterfeit.

The Sovereignty of Spiritual Relations

"I beseech thee for *my child*."

The Apostle might have spoken of Onesimus in many ways at this point, but he selects a word than which none could possibly be more binding or endearing.

How great this utterance is we may judge by imagining Paul to have written, "I beseech thee for *thy slave.*" That, of course, would immediately have recalled to the memory of Philemon all that was offensive, and might have steeled his heart against anything that the Apostle had further to say.

But Paul does not yet relate Onesimus to Philemon, but only to himself, and that, in the most endearing way.

There are two words in the New Testament translated "child"; one, παις, means a child in legal relation, and is translated "servant" in many places (e.g., Luke 15:26). The other, τεκνον, means a child by natural descent and is derived from the verb, τικτω, "to bear," "to bring forth children."

You will readily see that the latter word points to a relation much more vital and dear than the former, and it is the latter word which Paul uses here. He follows it up immediately by the words, "whom I have begotten"; and this verb is the one used of women bringing forth children (γενναω). There was not a word in his vocabulary which could have expressed more powerfully Paul's estimate of the new relation, or more tenderly his own affection for the runaway slave.

Such an utterance would altogether disarm Philemon of objection to receive back Onesimus. He would feel that to refuse to recognize the new situation and relation would almost de-Christianize him.

But the significance of this utterance passes —

beyond Paul and Onesimus and Philemon — to us. It tells of the sovereignty of spiritual relations: generally, of the vital relation of all believers to one another; and particularly, of the closeness of the bond which binds the soul-winner to the souls he wins.

This conviction and affection were ever strong in Paul. Writing to the Galatians, he says, "My little children, of whom I am again in travail until Christ be formed in you" (4:19). How different is the sentiment of Moses recorded in Numbers 11:12. The whole difference between two dispensations is reflected in these passages.

When shall we learn that "in Christ Jesus is neither Jew nor Greek; bond nor free" (Galatians 3:29)? Distinctions of race, education, social standing, or wealth cannot sever or weaken the link which binds all Christians to one another. British and African, learned and ignorant, rich and poor, prince and peasant, master and slave, are brothers and sisters "in Christ Jesus."

Christianity recognizes the fact of social distinctions, but does away with the tyranny and offensiveness of them in the life of the Church. Spiritual relations are sovereign.

But this verse teaches still more.

The Fruitful Possibilities of Trouble

"My child, whom I have begotten in my bonds."

One need not be idle because he is bound. When God's servants are bound, His Spirit and Word are not; spiritual children may then be born to them. Captivity may be eminently liberating and affliction wonderfully productive.

If we believe that our lives are plans of God, we shall look differently at our troubles, and more often turn them into triumphs.

A man's influence may be wider as his sphere is more circumscribed. In bonds we may give birth to Christian brethren.

It was good that Paul was imprisoned, if only to give birth to Onesimus, and to write this letter which has so profoundly affected the thought and action of Christendom.

Our very death-throes may become birth-pangs; our crushing may mean a new creation.

The thought in the next verse may be summarized as,

2. PAST AND PRESENT (11)

"Who was once unprofitable to thee, but now is profitable to thee and me."

Attention is here called to three points:

The Unprofitableness of the Unconverted

Paul speaks of Onesimus as having been "unprofitable." This refers, probably, not only to the offensive act, but to his whole service, reflecting, as it did, his character.

This is another tactful touch. Philemon might be beginning to think that Paul had not taken a serious enough view of the slave's offense; but Paul anticipates that, and makes it plain that he is fully aware of the sinfulness of the man's sin. He was a good-for-nothing and a bad-for-anything.

In thus describing Onesimus, Paul describes us all. Our Lord spoke even of those who did their duty as "unprofitable" (Luke 17:10); how worthless, then, must they be who do not even that!

We have "together become unprofitable." The verb ἀχρειοομαι, occurs here only (Romans 3:12) in the New

Testament; the substantives ἀχρεῖος only in Matthew 25:30 and Luke 17:10; and ἀχρῆστος only in our text. Unprofitable! Yes, that describes all who are out of Christ, even though they may make profession of Him, as did the man with one talent (Matthew 25:30).

Nothing is really to profit that does not serve the divine purpose and is not according to God's good pleasure. We are all Onesimuses in this respect. Solemn reflection! But the verse does not leave us there. It goes on to give hope through:

The Transforming Power of the Gospel

"Who once was . . . but now is."

This is a thoroughly Pauline expression. In Romans 6:21, we have, *"then. . .now";* and in Ephesians 2:12-13, we read: *"at that time* ye were without Christ. . .*but now, . . .";* and here, Onesimus "was *once* unprofitable . . . but *now. . .*"

This is the wonderful story of the possible becoming actual, of the sinful past being reversed, of the sinner being made a son.

No class was so degraded as the slaves of Paul's day; and, no doubt, Onesimus was typical of his kind, a liar, a thief, and treacherous. Yet, here he is, the worthless runaway, made profitable to his master and to Paul.

How was such an amazing change brought about? By the Gospel, which was and is "the power of God unto salvation to everyone who believes." Well does Maclaren say:

Christianity knows nothing of hopeless cases. It professes its ability to take the most crooked stick and bring it straight, to flash a new power into the blackest carbon, which will turn it into a diamond. Every duty will be done better by a man if he has the love and grace of Jesus Christ in his heart. New motives are brought into play, new powers are given, new standards of duty are set up. The small tasks become great, and the unwelcome sweet, and the difficult easy, when done for and through Christ. Old vices are crushed in their deepest source; old habits driven out by the force of a new affection, as the young leaf-buds push the withered foliage from the tree. Christ can make any man over again, and does so re-create every heart that trusts Him. Such miracles of transformation are wrought today as truly as of old.

This must be the confidence of us all as we go forth in the service of Christ, that His arm can reach the outermost and undermost, and save to the uttermost. If ever we are tempted to wonder if God can save some persons, let us read his letter again, and especially these words. "Who once was unprofitable . . . but now is profitable." But this verse has another value which we should not overlook.

The Apostle's Sense of Humor

Onesimus means *profitable.* But he belied the promise of his name. Great importance was attached to names in Bible times, and frequently these were changed. For example, Jacob to Israel, Simon to Peter. In this case the name was all right. It was the nature that was wrong. Onesimus did not need a new name, but he did need to live up to the one he had.

It is a disclosure of the rich and sane humanity of Paul that, at this most critical point in his communication, he should indulge in this playfulness. It is recorded of

Whitefield that on one occasion, from the pulpit, he made an appeal to one Shuter, a comedian, who had often played the character of Ramble. The preacher's words were, "And thou, poor *Ramble*, who hast so often *rambled* from Him, oh, end thy *ramblings* and come to Jesus."

So, here, Paul says to Philemon, *"Profitable* has up to now been *unprofitable* to you, but I will promise you that from now, if you will receive him back, he will be true to his name."

Someone has said that the only human quality not reflected in the Bible is humor. It is evident that the person who said that had no sense of humor. In many places in both Testaments, where it is not obvious in our translations, there is a playfulness such as we have here, which gives point and effect to purpose.

How saving is a sense of humor! How powerful a little playfulness may be! Be sorry for the man who has not somtimes a twinkle in his eye and a laugh in his voice, who never drops a joke from his pen. It is well not to be always grave on the way to the grave.

Another beautiful thought is to the effect that Onesimus was

3. SENT TO BE RECEIVED (12)

"Whom I have sent back to thee in his own person, that is, my very heart" (RV).

"Whom I have sent again; thou therefore received him, that is, mine own bowels" (AV).

The text here seems to reflect the emotion of the writer. He was sending Onesimus back, but not without a struggle. Paul begins to ask Philemon to receive Onesimus, but "in the swift rush of his thoughts" he forgets to do so until he gets to verse 17. The A. V. supplies the sentence which, however, is without textual authority.

What was in the Apostle's mind we can fairly gather from these two versions.

The Apostle's Identification of Himself with the Slave

"My very heart."

The word here employed, σπλαγχνα , refers to the viscera, which the Greeks distinguished as nobler and lower, the nobler viscera being the seat of the affections. The Hebrews, who did not make this distinction, regarded the bowels as the seat of emotion and affection. The A.V. follows the Hebrew idea, and the R.V. the Greek idea.

Either way, no word could be used to express more completely the thought of identification.

Onesimus was Paul's very heart; or, as he says in verse 17, "myself." Only a large and generous nature could speak this way, and of such an one; and in doing so Paul reminds us of Him Who said, "He that receives you, received Me." There is no more wonderful truth in the New Testament than that of the Savior's identification with sinners in His death and the believer's identification with Him in His risen life.

It is that great truth apprehended and believed that will lead to a fuller and richer fellowship among all believers, regardless of superficial and temporary distinctions.

But, we may also learn from this verse a lesson on,

The Resumption of Neglected Duties

"Sent back in his own person."

Think for a moment, not of the fact that Paul sent Onesimus back, but of that still more remarkable fact that Onesimus *went back.*

Here is an extraordinary thing! A slave, a criminal, deliberately going back to the master whom he had robbed and from whom he had run away, not knowing what kind of reception he would get: at best, going back to the slave's yoke.

Could anything better demonstrate the reality of his conversion than that?

To say that, because slavery is anti-Christian, Onesimus was under no obligation to return is to wholly miss the significance of his action.

Slavery was not then believed to be anti-Christian, nor for long centuries after. By the law of the times Onesimus belonged to Philemon in the relation of slave to master, and when the runaway went back, he was only doing his plain duty. You may say, "Then what was wonderful about it?" Two things: first, that he recognized it to be his duty; and, second, that he acted upon it.

Many more enlightened people than he do not always apprehend their duty; and many more, who know what is right, do it not.

One of the surest evidences of the presence of grace in the heart is the resumption of neglected duties; a return to the things from which we have run away. The man out of whom a legion of demons was cast besought Jesus that he might itinerate with Him; but Jesus said, "Go home." Jonah was bidden go East to Nineveh; but he went West towards Tarshish, and the Lord dealt with him. Upon repentance and restoration his duty still pointed to

Nineveh, and there he had to go. The sad experiences our disobedience brings upon us do not cancel the evaded duties which occasioned them. Neglected duties must be gone back to.

This verse raises also the momentous matter of:

The Attitude of Christianity to Slavery

"Whom I have sent back."

Now we think not so much of the fact that Onesimus went back, as that *Paul* sent him back. The great Apostle to the Gentiles, the church's first theologian, and the proclaimer of the Gospel of the soul's emancipation, deliberately sends a Christian brother back to slavery.

This raises a subject of first rate importance, on which this little letter throws a flood of light. Neither here nor anywhere in the New Testament is slavery directly condemned; nor, perhaps, were all the implications of the Christian Gospel apprehended by the apostles! Yet, beyond all question, slavery is anti-Christian, a sin against God, and treason toward man.

The time had not come, in Paul's day, for slavery's abolition, nor was society ready for such an advance for centuries after Paul; but in the New Testament are laid down those principles which were bound ultimately to destroy that nefarious traffic. Historically it is true that, as Christianity has grown, slavery has withered.

This veiled yet unmistakable attitude of the New Testament towards slavery is also its attitude towards all un-Christian institutions; it is the uncompromising antagonist of all the miserable anomalies of our present civilization.

Its triumphs, however, are not by way of revolution, but of reformation. The truth enlightens the conscience;

then political and social abuses disappear. So Paul sent Onesimus back to slavery. This is expressed in the simple but impressive words, of the next paragraph.

THE DESIRE (13-14)

1. "I WOULD HAVE KEPT . . . BUT" (13)

"Whom I would fain have kept with me, that in thy behalf he might minister unto me in the bonds of the Gospel."

Having definitely requested Philemon to receive back Onesimus, Paul now tells his friend of the conflict which had been going on in his own heart. He is not sending Onesimus back because he was anxious to get rid of him. Far, far from it! How gladly would he have kept him. Why, then, did he not keep him? That is the subject of these verses.

The text is worth studying at close quarters, for the words have been selected with great care. In the verse before us (13), there is a declaration, followed by an explanation; a desire, followed by a reason.

The Desire

"Whom I would have retained with me" (AV).

"Whom I would fain have kept with me" (RV).

The Apostle had come to love the slave. As Philemon was dear to Paul, so was Onesimus, and for the same reason, both were his converts. What Paul saw was not the difference between them socially, educationally, materially, but the sovereign fact that they, with him, were one in Christ Jesus.

No doubt Onesimus had become very attached to Paul.

Even slaves have hearts, and their love and loyalty are secured by kindness and trust, and not by suspicion and cruelty. This is not to say that Philemon had been cruel to Onesimus, but he was his master, and the relationship did not allow of his doing what a stranger might do. We are not necessarily the best people to deal, in spiritual things, with the members of our own household.

Here, then, Paul tells Philemon of the longing he had to keep with him the man whom he has sent away.

The order of the words is striking. "Whom I was desiring with myself to keep." The verb "to keep" is worthy of notice in connection with another verb in verse fifteen, "thou shouldst receive" (AV) "thou shouldst have" (RV).

The significance of this conjunction of words is observable not so much in the translation as in the original. Both are the verb ἐχω , "to hold"; with a preposition prefixed. In verse 13, the preposition is κατα, and in verse 15, it is ἀπο. Ἐχω with κατα means "to hold down," i.e. "to detain," or "to retain"; and ἐχω with ἀπο means "to have in full what is due."

Without doubt, Paul intentionally sets these words over against one another. It is as though he had said, "Him I would fain *detain:* but I know he is yours to *retain";* or, "Much did I desire to hold Onesimus, but I had not the right to do so as he was your property."

Another striking word in this sentence we shall notice in a moment. This expression of desire is immediately followed by:

The Reason

"That in thy stead he might have ministered unto me in the bonds of the Gospel" (AV).

"That in thy behalf he might minister . . ." (RV).

How pregnant a sentence is this! In these ten Greek words three things are said.

Onesimus would have been useful to Paul. "That he might serve me." Paul had a choice of words here, expressive of service, and he deliberately refuses the lowest δουλεύω , which means "to serve as a slave"; and chooses the highest διακονέω from which our word "*deacon*" comes, and which refers to ministry in every form. It is as though the Apostle had said, "Fain would I have made *your slave my deacon.*"

We can readily understand how useful Onesimus could have been to Paul. It had been his business to wait upon his master, to anticipate his every wish, and to be swift to perform it. These qualifications under the control of grace would make a man very useful to such a person as Paul, especially in the circumstances.

And this leads to the second thought here, namely, *Paul was in special need of a faithful servant.* "In the bonds of the Gospel." He was a sufferer, a captive; he was among strangers, people not predisposed towards him; he was old and worn and in need of loving attention. A faithful dog would be a great comfort to a man so placed; but a Christian servant, passionately devoted, would be a priceless treasure. He would attend to Paul's food; he would ease his chain; he would assist with his ablutions, and in every way attend to his wants.

In many ways the Phrygian slave would be better qualified to minister to the prisoner's wants than would his friends around him. And Onesimus would do this the more readily and gladly because Paul's bonds were occasioned by his faithfulness to that Gospel which had reached and rescued even such as he.

But there is yet another thought here: *Paul would have accepted Onesimus as Philemon's substitute.* "In thy stead: in thy behalf; for thee." This is a bold and confident word, and would greatly impress Philemon. Paul virtually says, "Philemon, I know that if you were here you would gladly minister to my need. That, of course, is impossible; but fain was I to keep your servant that he might do for me what I know you would have done."

And does Paul here hint at what is more plainly said in verse 19, namely, that Philemon was under some obligation to him, and, no doubt, would be quite willing to help discharge it in this way?

In all this Paul was winding Onesimus around Philemon's heart as he had wound him around his own. The threads were of delicate silk, and any one of them might easily have been snapped; but together they made a web which fast bound the slave to his master in a new relationship.

These words, so courteous and persuasive, were certain to procure a cordial reception for the returning fugitive.

In the preceding clause, Onesimus was spoken of as, in some sense, part of the Apostle's very self. In this, he is regarded as, in some sense part of Philemon. So he is a link between them. Paul would have taken his service as if it had been his master's. Can the master fail to take him as if he were Paul?

The Apostle has now told Philemon plainly what he would have done, and why he would have done it. Why then, did he not do it? This question is answered in the next verse, which is connected with this one by the word *but*.

2. "But You Had Not Given" (14)

"But without thy mind I would do nothing; that thy goodness should not be as of necessity, but of free-will".

Here we see how perfect a Christian gentleman Paul

was. He had an inborn sense of the fitness of things, which had been enriched and made more sensitive by the operations of grace.

In the previous verse Paul stated his desire and reason. Here he makes known his resolve and motive.

The Resolve

"Without thy mind I would do nothing."

Though Paul was eager to keep Onesimus, he would not do so without Philemon's knowledge and consent, spoken of here as his "mind." We have no right to extort benefits from our friends against their will. When friendship is presumed upon, we are to that extent untrue to its highest ideal.

The whole point of this utterance must be found in the verb translated "I would," brought into conjunction with the verb in the previous verse also translated "I would." These are not the same verbs in the original; neither are they in the same tense. Only by observing these facts can we rightly apprehend the Apostle's meaning. What he really says is, "I could have wished to keep Onesimus with me, but I had scruples, and so definitely willed to send him back to you."

The transition is here from the inner sphere of undecided inclinations to the definite act of determination which conducts to the sphere of fact.

Mark the difference between Paul's *wishing*, and his *willing*. The one tells of desire; the other of determination; the former points to his reflection; the latter, to his resolve.

If we are true to God and to ourselves, we may often will what we do not wish; and we may often wish what it would not be right to will. The former was the apostle's case. Paul wished one thing and willed another. He wished to keep Onesimus; but he willed to send him back to his master.

The best of Christians sometimes have a struggle between desire and resolve. Blessed are they who surrender their *wish* to God's *will*.

But a further point of interest and importance is found in the tenses of these verbs. Lightfoot says, "The imperfect implies a tentative, inchoate process; while the aorist describes a definite and complete act. The will stepped in and put an end to the inclinations of the mind."

Paul's wishing covered a period of time, but his willing occupied but the moment of his decision. His preference never crystallized into a definite purpose. He laid aside personal considerations and convenience in the interests of what was right.

Why did he will to do nothing without Philemon's consent? Several reasons have been given: First, grave penalties were pronounced by Roman law upon those who received or retained fugitive slaves. Second, he did not want to seem to keep back something which was due to Philemon, perhaps to his injury; of which, perhaps, Philemon might have complained. Third, Onesimus himself chose to go back, in order that he might show conclusively that he had not embraced the Christian religion as an excuse to withdraw himself from the power of his lawful lord. Finally, the Gospel would not be by this means slandered, as if under its pretext slaves might withdraw themselves with impunity from their masters.

All these were powerful reasons why Onesimus should go back to Colossae; and why Paul should will something other than he wished. But a less sensitive and conscientious person might easily have made a wrong decision for lack of wisdom or courage.

Do you think through to your decisions, putting mere preference and convenience on the one side, and justice and wisdom on the other, yielding always to the greater claim?

Paul, having made known his resolve, now discloses the motive which led him to this decision.

The Motive

"That thy goodness should not be as of necessity, but of free-will."

Two great words are here brought together, *necessity* and *free-will.* The power of the one is law, and of the other, love. There is the whole distance here between compulsion and spontaneity, between the dictates of duty and the desire which is delight.

There were three courses open to Paul in this matter: He could keep Onesimus with him and justify his action by the belief that Philemon would like him to do so. Or, he could retain Onesimus, meanwhile write to Philemon expressing his desire, and say that he would eagerly await his friend's reply. Or, he could say how useful Onesimus would be to him and what an affection he had for him, but that it was only right that he should go back to his master, and so he had sent him.

This last is the course Paul took, and it was the course of a Christian gentleman. Had he taken either of the other alternatives, Philemon's consent would certainly have been extorted. But Paul had far too much regard alike for civil rights and individual free-will.

Yet how delicately does he state the matter. He does not say that the good which Philemon would have done his prisoner-friend by proxy, had he kept Onesimus, would have been of necessity, that would have been uncharitable to Philemon's good nature; but he adds a small word of only two letters which gives an entirely different complexion to the remark: "That thy goodness might not be *as* of necessity." By this he meant, "I will not suppose that it would really be by constraint; but it must not even wear the appearance of being so" (Lightfoot).

The difference this little word makes in the sense may be seen by a reference to 2 Corinthians 11:17, where it is used in the same way: "That which I speak, I speak not after the Lord, but *as* in foolishness." The Apostle does not say that he is speaking foolishly; he is not; but that it *would seem* to some that he was doing so.

That is the force of the word in our text, and its employment is but an added evidence of the Apostle's consummate tact.

May we not find here a fundamental condition and principle of Christian service? It is true that the Lord commands His servants, but the service which we yield Him must be glad and free, the spontaneous expression of our heart's love, "not as of necessity, but willingly."

But what is true of all service is true of all conduct. Jerome from this passage justly deduces as a conclusion that Paul held the principle that "nothing in moral action is good which is not voluntary," and he makes a striking application of this principle. This necessity of voluntariness in order to right moral action is fatal to fatalism.

THE SITUATION (15-17)

The Apostle has plainly made *request* that Onesimus be taken back (verses 10-12), and has also disclosed the *desire* that for a time had possession of him (verses 13-14). He now, in repeating the request, bids Philemon acknowledge and accept the *situation*.

What then exactly is the situation?

In verses 15-17 Paul says three things, and so says them as to render them applicable in fields and to circumstances far removed from those which gave them rise.

1. THE WAY OF PROVIDENCE (15)

"For, perhaps, he was therefore parted from thee for a season, that thou shouldest have him for ever."

Here are but eleven Greek words and it is amazing how much truth and tenderness are communicated by them. Let us take in order the several thoughts as they come.

"For"

The word *for* connects the verse with what precedes, and it makes what Paul is about to say another reason why he had set aside his wish and had willed to send Onesimus back. That reason is that God, in permitting the flight of Onesimus, may have had Philemon's own interests in view.

Each word in this verse has a force of its own, which we must briefly notice. The Apostle says:

"He Was Therefore Parted From Thee"

Commentators, following Chrysostom, observe that Paul does not say, "for this cause *he fled*," but "for this cause *he was parted.*" This other statement would have been true, but it would also have been ugly; moreover, it was not Paul's object to emphasize Onesimus' offence now that he had repented and was willing to return, so he uses this euphemism in the interests alike of tact and grace.

But there is more than that. Paul does not say, *"He*

parted from thee," but *"he was parted."* The verb is passive not active. Of course, the slave voluntarily went away, but the Apostle sees much more in it than that, and it is what he sees which gives this verse its chief value.

Tennyson says,

> Oh yet we trust —
> That not a worm is cloven in vain;
> That not a moth with vain desire
> Is shrivell'd in a fruitless fire,
> Or but subserves another's gain.

Back of those words lies a great truth, the truth of providence. Onesimus had robbed his master and had run away. There was, probably, no extenuating circumstance. The lot of this youth was infinitely better than that of his kind, seeing he had had a Christian for a master; but, instead of displaying gratitude, he presumed upon Philemon's goodness, robbed him, and absconded. Verily he was guilty and richly deserved punishment.

Paul would have been the first to admit all this; yet, it is not that point of view that he here takes, but quite another, startling and arresting. He virtually says, "The sin of that youth of yours is not to be in vain. Behind it is a power which will harness it to divine purpose — a chemistry by means of which the vile and worthless will be transmuted into beauty and use."

When Onesimus ran away, nothing was less likely than that he should ever make good. At first sight, it would seem morally impossible that his evil should be made to serve any worthy end.

Yet so it was, as Paul here affirms. And what is true in this instance is true all the time and everywhere. One of the greatest utterances in the Bible is the riddle which

Samson propounded: "Out of the eater came forth meat, and out of the strong came forth sweetness" (Judges 14:14).

That is not only the key to the Book of the Judges, but to the whole of divine revelation and all history. For example: the relation of believers to Christ is now more intimate than it could ever have been had Adam and Eve not fallen. Yet how damnable was their sin!

Think of the incalculable good that came out of the selling of Joseph by his brethren! He himself said, "As for you, ye meant evil against me; *but God meant it for good,* to bring to pass, as it is this day, to save much people alive" (Genesis 50:20). Yet these brothers stand branded for all time.

We shall not forget what were the historical consequences of Moses slaying the Egyptian. He fled from death into the desert, where he was disciplined, instructed, and equipped for the great deliverance of his people from Egyptian bondage. Without that training it would appear that he could never have wrought that work; and yet what likelihood was there of his ever having left the Court for the desert, except under some such compulsion as this?

How contemptibly wicked was the sin of David, a sin which has for thirty centuries caused the enemies of the Lord to blaspheme. Yet, out of that, utterance was given to the remorse and repentance of his broken heart, which has become, ever since, the language of the penitent. Psalm 51: "Create in me a clean heart, oh God; and renew a right spirit within me."

No one will be disposed to make any excuse for Judas which his conscience would not allow him to make for himself; yet, think of the inestimable blessings which have flowed from his cursed crime!

The Jews must bear full responsibility for having stoned

Stephen, and thus, for having instituted the Martyr's Roll. But the providential end served by their cruelty is patent on every succeeding page of the record. It was the beginning of the great outspreading which shall not cease until all the world has learned of Christ.

It would be easy to add to these Bible illustrations numberless others from the history of the Church. But enough. This great truth stands demonstrated, that God is ever making the wrath of men to praise Him; thus, divine purposes may be discerned shining through questionable human acts, and that divine ends are accomplished by means of, as well as in spite of, the sins of men.

It cannot be emphasized too strongly that the sinner will be held accountable for his sin, and that he can take no credit to himself for any good that, in the providence of God, may come of it. Yet the fact remains, written large on the page of history, that God makes all things serve his ends.

The greatest crime that is laid at the door of man has become the greatest blessing to mankind. The Cross of Calvary is at once our doom and our hope. Out of that darkness has come universal light. Out of that bondage has come glorious liberty. Out of that death has come eternal life.

It would be but vain speculation to inquire, what would have happened, if these evils had not been perpetrated. Two facts stand outside all speculation, and beyond all question, namely, that sin is inexcusable and will be judged, and that God, in addition to ruling over all, overrules all.

So much then, is in this simple phrase. Yet, we have by no means exhausted the fulness of this verse. Paul adds:

"For Perhaps."

Paul does not question for a moment the general truth above stated, but he would be cautious in the application of it. We certainly cannot always trace the ways of God; these are often past finding out; but we must not therefore deny that He is in the affairs of men fulfilling eternal designs.

It is well, however, for us to be cautious in our interpretation of events and applications of the great principle. MacIaren says "*Perhaps* is one of the hardest words for minds of a certain class to say, but in regard to all such subjects and to many more, it is the motto of the wise man, and the shibboleth which sifts out the patient modest lovers-of-truth from rash theorists and precipitate dogmatizers. Impatience of uncertainty is a moral fault which mars many an intellectual process."

"That Thou Shouldest Have Him"

We have already observed the conjunction of this verb $\dot{\alpha}\pi\epsilon\chi\epsilon\iota\nu$ with that other in verse 13, $\kappa\alpha\tau\epsilon\chi\epsilon\iota\nu$, the one there meaning *to retain*, and the one here, *to restore*. He who has parted should now *be restored*.

Paul suggests that the underlying purpose of the sinful departure was a return which would mean that Philemon would possess Onesimus more fully than otherwise he could possibly have done.

This thought stands unmistakable in the accompanying words,

"For an Hour . . . Eternally"

"Perhaps he was parted from thee for a season, that thou shouldest have him for ever."

The eternal consequence was in that "hour." How much happened in so short a time! The passing moment determined the future millenniums. The temporary loss was everlasting gain.

We must not limit the sense of *eternally* here. It does not mean that Philemon may now reckon upon his slave remaining with him, upon his having him in permanent servitude (Leviticus 25:46; Exodus 21:6), but that Onesimus and Philemon, both having eternal life, were eternally related to one another. The expression connects this life with the next and intimates that spiritual bonds are indissoluble. This man was "parted for a season to be possessed for ever."

Has this not been the story of many? Augustine ran away to this same Rome from Monica and nearly broke her heart; but as a result of his waywardness and wickedness, she before long received him again forever in the bonds of new birth. It is the story of every prodigal who returns. Death does not dissolve our relations in Christ Jesus. When we return to God, we return to one another in all relations that are true and abiding. The *season* of Onesimus' absence had secured for him a share in the eternal communion of saints, because it secured for him a place in the heart of the Eternal.

We should not rest content with recognizing the general truth, but ever make conscious effort to feel that *this passing instant* has something to do with our eternal character and with our eternal destiny.

Paul now goes on to define the new relationship.

2. THE SLAVE AND BROTHER (16)

"No longer as a servant, but more than a bond-servant, a brother beloved, specially to me, but how much rather to thee, both in the flesh and in the

Lord."

The relation between the slave and the master is new not only in its *duration* (verse 15), but in its *quality* (verse 16). Paul says, not only *that* they are forever related, but *how* they are related.

"A Bond-Slave" (δοῦλος)

Observe that now for the first time he is plainly referred to as a "slave." Paul had spoken of him as his "child" and as his "very heart" (verses 10, 12), avoiding any reference to his servitude because, until now, it did not suit his purpose. But now it does; and he uses the word only to bring it into relation with another, the "brother" of this same verse.

"No Longer as a Bond-Slave"

Paul does not say "no longer a bond-slave." He was not sending Onesimus back to Philemon with request that he be manumitted. Oh no. Onesimus is returning to his place and duties as before, yet, with a difference; and so, Paul says, "no longer *as* a slave." In matter of fact and outwardly he is still to be a slave, yet no longer is he to be regarded as that, for he is "no longer" merely that.

The objective negative here employed, οὐκέτι , not μηκέτι , means that whatever Philemon, or anyone else may think about it, it is a matter of positive fact that Onesimus is a freeman of Christ and, therefore, is no longer *as* a slave.

What Paul virtually said to his friend was, "Onesimus' condition does not depend upon your conception of it, only I would have you recognize what that condition is and act accordingly."

Here, then, are two great truths: First, conversion to God does not release men from their civil, social, and commercial bonds; we still have offices to fill and duties to perform according to our calling and ability. And second, conversion to God will enable us to accomplish these tasks from a new motive and in a better manner; and, where Christians are concerned, all our relations will be adjusted and adorned in the light of the fact that we are "one in Christ Jesus." Paul makes this quite plain in the next clause.

"More Than a Bond-Slave, a Brother Beloved"

When Paul says "more than," he means that Onesimus was still a slave but no longer that only or merely. What then was he more? "A brother beloved."

Slave and brother! What a juxtaposition! the slave-brother! That is a revolutionary and revolutionizing idea, an idea which eighteen hundred years have scarcely served to get into our hearts and minds.

It is the Glad News of Christ's redeeming sacrifice, and that alone, which can make slaves and masters to be brothers, which can overleap all racial and social distinctions and bring men together in a common fellowship.

Paul goes on to say, "Onesimus is a brother beloved, most of all to me, but more than most of all to thee, (if that be possible)." By this, the fact that Onesimus is Philemon's slave is not a drawback but an advantage, now that he is a Christian, binding him more closely to his master in holy brotherhood than he can be bound to anyone else.

But there is yet another word added.

"Both in the Flesh and in the Lord"

What exactly is meant by this? The most natural thought is that which makes "in the flesh" to mean in the earthly and personal relations of common life, and "in the Lord" to signify the spiritual and religious relationships of worship and the Church. In this view natural feeling and supernatural communion are harmonized, and the spheres to which they belong are vitally related.

This is a great truth, too little practiced. Many professing Christians are quite willing to regard their Christian subordinates "in the Lord" on Sundays, but insist on regarding them "in the flesh" all the rest of the week. It has been said that "some good people seem to keep their brotherly love in the same wardrobe with their Sunday clothes." These things ought not so to be. Class distinctions and snobbishness among Christians are an abomination unto the Lord; yet sadly there is much of these.

It is only in the Lord that all our social relations can be properly adjusted and regulated, preserved from abuse alike by the master and the servant, the employer and the employee, the sovereign and the subject.

But another significance has been given to these words. Some understand them as implying that Onesimus and Philemon were both Gentiles, and therefore rightly termed "brothers in the flesh," which Paul, who was a Jew could scarcely say.

It has even been suggested that Onesimus was the natural brother of Philemon, the child of the same father, by a different mother, a slave. This is conjectured from the fact that it was usual with the Phrygians to sell their children, and one might be the slave of the other in the civil relation.

This interpretation is possible, but the former one is

certain, and is as binding on us today as it was on Philemon long ago.

"In the flesh" Philemon had the brother for a slave; and "in the Lord" he had the slave for a brother.

3. THE DEPUTY PARTNER (17)

All the Apostle's tact and tenderness are again in evidence here. The language he employs is such as to make it impossible for his friend to deny him his request.

This request he wished to make in verse 12, but did not do so. There he said, "whom I have sent back to thee in his own person." But here, he says right out, "receive him." He does not say, "reinstate," but "receive," a much more tender word. Then again, he puts in the personal plea, "as myself." Paul is sure Philemon would receive *him*, he wishes therefore that that welcome should be extended to Onesimus.

What more could he have asked for anyone?

Yet all this he asks for one who was regarded as the very least. This is what grace does in the hearts of men.

There is one other touch in this plea which would carry, and was intended to carry, great weight with Philemon. Paul says, "If then thou countest me a partner."

There is first of all the word *partner*, that is, comrade. Throughout the letter Paul has carefully avoided any exercise of his apostolic authority. Not on that ground does he appeal, but on this: that he is old, that he is a prisoner, and now, that he is a partner with Philemon, having common feelings, interests, and hopes, a sharer with him of the faith that is in Christ Jesus.

This reference is far-reaching, and, if it be acknowledged by Philemon, commits him to all that Paul has asked and to much more.

If these two are yoked together they will act together.

That is the essential idea of partnership. Comrades in conflict, partners in business, sharers in service, have common ideas and aims; they are united in principle and purpose, however they may differ in method, or they are not comrades, partners, sharers at all.

Do we not find here the secret of success and the cause of failure in the Christian enterprise? Success, wherever this partnership is acknowledged and acted upon; failure, wherever it is not.

If the churches have exposed themselves to the criticism, not to say to the ridicule, too often, of the ungodly, it is because petty jealousy has taken the place of Christian sympathy, and miserable rivalry the place of hearty co-operation. If we are ever to succeed we must beckon to the other ships to come and help us land the cargo.

Observe how delicately Paul puts the matter. He does not say, "I am partner with you, so receive Onesimus as myself," but, "If thou holdest me to be a comrade."

He will not assume anything that would be to his own advantage; but he puts it to Philemon. Yet he knows full well how deep and true is Philemon's love for him, and is quite confident of the comradeship, but Paul is too great a man to presume or insist. He so utterly trusts what is true and right, that at the feet of these he lays everything and waits. That should be a rebuke to the rash haste which is responsible for so many of our troubles.

THE PROMISE (18-19)

One wonders what more there is that Paul can say. Yet, in drawing his letter to a close he has one more word to write on behalf of Onesimus.

He has made the *request*, disclosed his once found *desire,* explained the *situation;* and now, having kept it to the last, he names Onesimus' sin, and takes, as far as one man can take for another, responsibility for it in its human ethical aspect. And so, we now have the *promise:*

But if he hath wronged thee at all, or oweth thee aught, put that to mine account.
I Paul write it with mine own hand, I will repay it: that I say not unto thee that thou owest to me even thine own self besides.

Paul's playfulness here becomes evident again. In somewhat formal fashion, he presents to Philemon a credit and debit account.

First of all he says,

1. "I OWE YOU" (18-19A)

Observe that now, for the first time, and quite plainly,

Paul Acknowledges Onesimus' Sin .

"But . . . aught."

The offence is first admitted, and then described: "Philemon, I know that Onesimus has wronged you, I know that he is in your debt." How did Paul know? Of course Onesimus had confessed all; under the action of the Spirit of God he had come to see his sin in its true light and to own up to the injury which he had done his master. If he had not done this, what evidence would there have been of repentance? There is no conversion where there is no confession, and where sin has been specific, confession must be also. Behind Paul's acknowledgment to Philemon is Onesimus' to him.

It is an acknowledgment of wrong, and of wrong in the form of robbery. Yet Paul will not use that ugly word, for that would tend to irritate Philemon. Paul speaks of a *debt,* and yet does not define the nature or extent of it.

The terms of this letter are perfectly magical, and the wonder of them consists quite as much in what Paul does not say as in what he does say. When Paul says "if," he is not implying any doubt; the case is stated hypothetically. That this youth had wronged his master was beyond question; yet there was no need to make the fact more bold than necessary.

But we must not forget that all sin is wrong; that is, it is a violation of law, an unjust act, an injury done to someone; it is negation of right. Under cover of that word *wrong* are the countless forms which sin may take. It may be killing, or stealing, or lying, or anything else, but all is wrong. Here, then, are two great words, *wrong* and *right,* under one or other of which everything may be classified. Right is the only true standard of conduct, and wrong is departure from it. All our action should be governed by the principle "Whether it is right in the sight of God" (Acts 4:19).

Paul's association of Onesimus with himself (verses 10, 12, 16-17) was not for one moment intended to minimize his former guilt, nor in any way or measure to excuse his offense. That is the force of "but" in verse 18: "Receive him as myself . . . but . . ." Paul would ever act in the light; he would have before him all the facts, and then he would judge righteous judgment.

And so we are prepared for this further, that

Paul Acknowledges Onesimus' Obligation and Takes It upon Himself.

"Put that to mine account."

This is his I.O.U. voucher to Philemon. Paul clearly recognized, what we sometimes fail to admit, that new life does not cancel old debt. The fact that Onesimus had become a Christian in nowise set him free from his moral obligations.

Neither does it set us free. The profession of conversion is no reason why you should not pay your debts, keep your promises, be diligent at your occupation, or make amends for previous wrongdoing. Such profession is an additional reason why you should do all these things. Christianity is nothing if it is not ethical. Yet there are many who look to their religion for sanction for most unethical conduct.

Paul goes beyond the legal requirement in this case. A slave had no standing in the eyes of the law; in the secular court he could neither be debtor nor creditor, properly speaking, as against his master.

But we all know that what is legally right may be morally wrong, and that what is legally wrong may be morally right. Conscience is greater than constitution, and the ethical sense, than legal enactments.

And so, in the Christian light Onesimus was given to see that he was under moral obligation to right the wrong, to make good to his master, in some way, the injury he had done him. But how was he to do this? The money he had stolen he had spent, he was a penniless slave; like the man in the parable, he had nothing to pay.

Now Paul, having brought Onesimus to think and will as he should in relation to the whole matter, steps in and makes himself bond. He says to Philemon, "I will repay the sum; see, I put my name, PAUL, to this undertaking; it shall be done."

What a wonderful heart Paul had, and what a faith in God. Both qualities are now exhibited. Here is a prisoner, dependent upon the gifts of others, undertaking to pay the debts of a runaway slave. Where was the money to come from? Was he allowed and able to earn some by the work of his hands? Or, was he going to pray it in?

Not for one moment are we to suppose that Paul made this promise in the belief that Philemon would not allow him to fulfil it. While Paul would expect that his friend would treat the whole matter with the generosity for which he was so well known (verses 4-7), he, nevertheless, did not presume upon that but quite seriously and purposefully took upon himself to clear this account.

In doing this, does he not remind us of another, Who, when we were in hopeless debt to God and had nothing to pay, undertook our case, paid our debt with His blood, and set us free?

> Jesus paid it all, all to Him I owe;
> Sin had left a crimson stain,
> He washed it white as snow.

We all are God's Onesimuses, and but for our Great Friend, what would have become of us?

2. "You Owe Me" (19b)

"That I say not unto thee that thou owest to me even thine own self besides."

Having undertaken to pay, Paul then reverses the matter. Paul is still thinking of a debt, but now of Philemon's to him, and not of Onesimus' to Philemon.

The word "to owe" in this verse is not the recurrence of the one in the previous verse. There it is ὀφείλω, but here, προσοφείλω, which means "to owe besides, or in addition." We naturally ask besides what? In addition to what? For answer we go to the first part of the sentence, "that I say not unto thee."

Lightfoot says that there is a suppressed thought here, which expressed, would have read, "I will repay it though indeed you cannot fairly claim repayment, for you owe me much more than Onesimus owes you, and, over and above that, your own self." All that had made life to Philemon gloriously worthwhile he owed instrumentally to Paul, who had led him to Christ. That debt Philemon could never pay and was not asked to pay, but it is suggested that he see in his own case his slave's case, and that as he had "freely received" he should "freely give" and forgive.

And this is the standard for us all. In a parable our Lord has solemnly warned us against refusing to forgive, we who have been forgiven — especially as anything which may be due to us is as nothing in comparison to what we owed God and were forgiven for Jesus' sake. Well may we pray, "forgive us our debts as we forgive our debtors."

RETREAT FROM THE OBJECT OF THE LETTER

Paul's Claim and Confidence of Love (20-21)

The Claim of Love (20)

1. The Favors Requested

2. The Sphere of Fulfillment

The Confidence of Love (21)

1. In Philemon's Obedience

2. In Philemon's Generosity

Verses 20-21

Yea, brother, let me have joy of thee in the Lord; refresh my heart in Christ. Having confidence in thine obedience I write unto thee, knowing that thou wilt do even beyond what I say.

5

RETREAT FROM THE OBJECT
OF THE LETTER. (20-21)

Paul's Claim and Confidence of Love

You will observe that as there was an approach to the object of this letter (8-9), so there is a retreat from it (20-21); the heart of the letter, the disclosure of the object, being in verses 10-19.

Observe also, that in neither the prologue, 1-9, nor the epilogue, 20-25, is there any mention of Onesimus. The Apostle's tender request in verses 10-19 is encircled by considerations human and divine, personal and relative, natural and spiritual, which were bound to go a long way towards securing the reinstatement of his runaway slave.

In several important respects the Apostle's closing thoughts return to those with which he opened, as a comparison of verses 20-21 with 8-9, 22 with 4-7, and 23-25 with 1-3 will show.

The first verse now before us makes a personal claim (20); and the second gives expression to an inspiring confidence (21); and both are in the embrace of love.

THE CLAIM OF LOVE (20)

"Yea, brother let me have help of thee in the Lord; refresh my heart in Christ."

Here we shall notice, first, the *favors requested* and

then, the *sphere* of *fulfilment*.

1. THE FAVORS REQUESTED

In introducing these requests, the Apostle says, "Yea, brother." The words are designed to be affectionate and appealing. Paul here calls Philemon what he wished Philemon to regard Onesimus to be, a brother (verse 16). There are only two brotherhoods of which we know anything: the brotherhood of race, which is all inclusive; and the brotherhood of grace, which embraces only the born-again children of God.

It is to the latter that Paul here points. Just because Philemon was a Christian, he was Paul's brother; and just because Onesimus was a Christian, he was Philemon's brother; and just because Paul was a Christian, he was Onesimus' brother, and so the circle is complete.

This is the entreaty of a brother to a brother on behalf of a brother. Paul does not ask Philemon to make it so, but only to recognize that it is so (verses 16-20). We are all so willing to recognize it as an idea, but so slow to act upon it as a fact.

Not more sure is the brotherhood of man in sin, than is the brotherhood of all believers in Christ, of whatever color, tongue, clime, or social status. It is well that, in drawing this letter to a close, Paul should again strike this note, for if this be recognized, all that it implies is carried.

Paul then requests two favors: he wishes *help* and *refreshing.*

The Request for Help

"Let me have help of thee."

This word, *help,* occurs nowhere else in the New Testament and almost certainly it is now used in a playful way, reminding Philemon of the meaning of his slave's name. *Onesimus* means *helpful* or *profitable;* and the verb is derived from ὀνίνημι , meaning "to help, to profit." Onesimus had not been true to his name; but Paul is quite sure that he is going to be. He has already said of him, "Who once was *unprofitable* to thee, but now is *profitable* to thee and to me" (verse 11).

To this thought the Apostle now gives quite a new turn and says in effect. "Philemon my brother, what Onesimus has been to me and is going to be to you, I want you to be to me. He is your Onesimus; will you be mine?"

We cannot all figure in some great role, but we can all help. You will remember that in the enumeration, in 1 Corinthians, of the gifts bestowed upon the Church is the gift, "helps" (12:28, not the same Greek word as in our text). How much this covers, and how indispensable it is! It is both a gift and a grace. The church that has most Onesimuses in it is doing the most.

We have a right to expect "help" not only from God (Hebrews 4:16, still another Greek word) but from one another, and this is something that we all can give.

Paul does not specify the kind of help he wants, so we may assume that what he is asking is satisfaction with reference to the subject of this letter. What he means, no doubt, is that if Philemon restores Onesimus, it will be helping him, his aged friend, far away and in prison. Would Philemon, could Philemon refuse such a request?

We see, therefore, that although Paul does not again directly refer to Onesimus, he is still in Paul's thoughts and desires.

The Request for Refreshing

"Refresh my heart."

This phrase takes us back to verse 7, where we read that Philemon had often refreshed the hearts of the saints. Paul believes that if Philemon had done this for others, he would not be slow to do it for him.

Lightfoot points out that this is a compound verb, ἀναπαύειν , that expresses a temporary relief, the simple verb expressing a final cessation. It has, therefore, the force of relaxation, or refreshment, as a preparation for the renewal of labor or suffering.

For Philemon to grant Paul his request would be a great encouragement to the latter; it would stimulate him to further service, in prison though he was. To know that Onesimus had been reinstated would be to the aged captive what a draught from a crystal spring would be to a thirsty traveler, what a meal would be to a hungry pilgrim.

We have said that it is in the power of all of us to help, and so it is to refresh; we help by refreshing, and we refresh by helping. A kindly word spoken in season, how good it is! The look or handshake of sympathy or appreciation, heartening it is! In the strength of such tokens of love the soldier will go forth to the fight, the workman to his task, and the pilgrim to the climb; such refreshing will make the lot of the captive easier, and the bed of the sufferer softer, and surely this is well worthwhile doing!

But how may it best be done? I would direct your attention here to:

2. THE SPHERE OF FULFILMENT

"In the Lord . . . In Christ."

Two interpretations may be given to these words in their present connection, and perhaps both were in the Apostle's mind. First, Christ is the sphere in which Philemon may help and refresh Paul, or in which the Apostle may be helped and refreshed. Second, Christ is the source from which the help and refreshing get their strength. Both interpretations are true, and we cannot afford to forget either. Help and refreshing which are not in and by Christ are, at best, poor and temporary.

"In Christ" carries in it the secret of all sweet humanities and beneficences; it is the spell which calls out fairest charity and is the only victorious antagonist of harshness and selfishness.

Taking the verse as a whole, we should observe the ground on which the final plea is made for Onesimus. It is not now because to receive him is *right,* but because to do so will *please* Paul.

Secondary motives must never be allowed to take the place of primary ones, but, on the other hand, the secondary must not be despised. Sometimes the latter succeed where the former fail, and any motives that are worthy at all should be employed to secure ends that are at all worthy.

Pleasing men may be mere obsequiousness, but to please Christ is the highest form of devotion. His ruling motive should be ours, "I do always those things which please Thee." To coldly obey a mere law of duty is one thing; and to joyfully gratify a living, loving Lord is quite another. We must obey, of course; but we must do more. Of whom is it said that they receive whatsoever they ask of God? Of those who "keep his commandments, and do the things that are *pleasing* in His sight" (1 John 3:22).

Paul, therefore, in this simple verse before us, sets forth a great truth and enunciates a great principle; and in passing from this, let us not forget that it is given to us to help and refresh Christ.

THE CONFIDENCE OF LOVE (21)

"Having confidence in thine obedience I write unto thee knowing that thou wilt do even beyond what I say."

This confidence, you will observe, is twofold. It is in Philemon's obedience and in his generosity.

1. CONFIDENCE IN PHILEMON'S OBEDIENCE

We observed, when considering verses 8-9, that throughout this note to Philemon, Paul deliberately sets aside, as a ground of appeal, his apostolic authority, and would move his friend to action by other motives.

Only for one moment is that attitude departed from, and it is here in his employment of the word *obedience;* and it is now so used as to be devoid of harshness. Paul's command is not that of duty, but of love; it is not that of a master but of a friend.

Paul has confidence in Philemon's obedience; he trusts him. No other word would have been so suitable here as this, for it kept the appeal up to the level on which it had moved all the time, and it would make an appeal to Philemon to which he and all of us ever feel we must respond — the appeal of trust, of loving expectation.

Obedience becomes easy and delightful when it is in response to trust and love, and if there were more of these latter, there would be less of disobedience.

But Paul goes further. He expresses his

2. CONFIDENCE IN PHILEMON'S GENEROSITY

"Knowing that thou wilt do even beyond what I say."

What is the Apostle thinking of in this remark? Is it a veiled request that Philemon release Onesimus from slavery? It may be so, for that everywhere is the undertone of this music; yet, he does not definitely make such a request.

The time had not come for the abolition of slavery, nor did it come on any considerable scale for long centuries after Paul's time; and in some lands it has not come yet. For Paul to have made such a request would, at that time, have raised a very great question; and had there been any concerted movement in that direction, it could only have issued in utter disaster for the slaves.

But perhaps Paul, by these words, does not intend more than to express his confidence that his friend will not barely accede to the request which he has made, but will do so gladly and generously.

"Men will do much to fulfil generous expectations." "Trust will act like a magnet to draw reluctant feet into the path of duty. A will which mere authority could not bend, like iron when cold, may be made flexible when warmed by this gentle heat." Where love commands, it is most likely that love will respond. The human heart will not rise to anything very heroic at the instigation of the law. Like attracts like; and so if we wish the most from anyone we must appeal to the highest in them out of the highest in ourselves.

In all of us there are slumbering heroisms only awaiting such a call. It is difficult to say which is the more gladsome part, to appeal or to respond. "A heart truly touched by the love of Jesus Christ will not seek to know the lowest limit of duty, but the highest possibility of service."

> Give what thou canst; high heaven rejects the lore of nicely calculated less or more.

The ground on which Paul appealed to Philemon is the same on which Christ appeals to us. *Where Sinai failed, Calvary triumphs.* There is nothing like the love of Christ to move to noble life and service; that is the note which goes down to our depths and calls up the worthiest response. If it does that in us when others sound it, it will do that in others when we sound it. If when making a true appeal we can add, "knowing that thou wilt do even beyond what I say," we may be confident that our confidence will not be in vain.

EXPECTATION

Philemon's Prayers for Paul

Paul's Hope of Liberation

1. The Source

2. The Ground

Paul's Request for Accommodation

1. His Modesty

2. His Motive

Verse 22

But withal prepare me also a lodging: for I hope that through your prayers I shall be granted unto you.

6

EXPECTATION (22)

Philemon's Prayers for Paul

You will observe that verse 22 and verses 4-7 go together. In the latter we have commendation, and here expectation. In the one the reference is to Paul's prayers for Philemon, but here it is to Philemon's prayers (and those of his household) for Paul. Though these lines were written quite artlessly, there is, nevertheless, a most striking correspondence between the various parts.

The Apostle is now drawing his letter to a close, but up to the last he has Onesimus in view. He is resolved that no line of appeal shall be unemployed that would help to secure a welcome back to the runaway slave; and though at the end as at the beginning, he speaks of matters quite personal, yet all is made contributory to the one end. So consider this closing appeal:

"But withal prepare me also a lodging: for I hope that through your prayers I shall be granted unto you."

We shall examine the second part of the verse first as the former part is entirely dependent upon it.

PAUL'S HOPE OF LIBERATION

1. THE GROUND OF HIS HOPE

"I hope that through your prayers"

Brief as that sentiment is, how much it contains! Observe one or two points:

Paul Believed in Praying.

Some of the richest passages in Paul's writings would be lost if his prayers and references to prayer were extracted. One has but to think of the prayers preserved in his prison epistles as proof of this; in Philippians the prayer for discerning love; in Colossians, written at the same time as this note to Philemon, the prayer for enlightened behavior; in Ephesians, those two great prayers, the one for spiritual illumination, and the other for divine plenitude.

The man who offered these believed in prayer and knew how to pray. He believed in prayer not only as subjectively beneficial, but as objectively effectual; not only as emotional, but as impetrative. He believed in prayer as a practical power.

How much Paul prayed for others we shall never know, nor how much he accomplished by his prayers. When Paul says, "my prayers," he is referring to something that was central and dynamic in his life.

Paul Depended on Prayer.

He tells Philemon that he is hoping to be set free from Rome because the household at Colossae were praying for him. No doubt he had been praying for himself, but he does not refer to that, for he wishes to impress Philemon and his circle with the importance of their intercessions; he would have them know how much he depended upon them. I say "them" because the "you" of the text is plural, not singular; Paul is not referring to the prayers of Philemon only, but of all those whom he named in verses one and two.

Are we at all awake to the importance of the prayers of other people for us? Do we sufficiently realize our debt, in this matter, to others? Times without number we have been blessed because others have prayed for us, and often when we were not praying for ourselves. We may suppose that at least as many souls have been saved as the result of praying as have been turned to God by preaching; and, I doubt not, many a preacher has received credit for conversions which really were the result of private prayers.

We can ask no greater service of any than that they pray for us; and we can do no greater service to any than to pray for them. If you would be a real blessing to anyone today, take his case to the Throne of Grace. If Paul depended on the prayers of others, well may we.

Paul was Cautious in Speaking of Answers to Prayers

He does not say, "I know," but "I hope that through your prayers I shall be granted unto you." He did not know that he would be released from Rome, even though he had been prayed for. Such deliverance was not dependent upon the wish of his friends but upon the will of God.

Paul did not believe that prayer is a means whereby we get God to do what we want, but whereby we get to know and are moved to do what God wills.

The will of God is the ground of prayer, and whether or not our actual requests are answered, if we have at all understood the nature and purpose of prayer, the exercise of it can never be in vain. If, behind all our petitions is, "not my will, but Thine be done," then our every prayer is answered.

Had Paul not been released from Rome he would not have supposed that the Colossian prayers had been unheeded, but only that they had been answered in a way other than was expected. The prayer of faith can only be offered where the will of God is not definitely known.

Peter's friends prayed that he might be released from prison, and he was. Do you suppose that the Church did not pray for Stephen? Yet he was martyred. In both instances the will of God was done, and in each instance there was surprise.

Paul says, "I hope." This word as commonly used may point to either aspiration or assurance. The Christian hope is always assurance; the hope of which we are not to be ashamed is not a fond desire, but a glad certainty. Its use in our text does not imply certainty, but only expresses desire; and in so speaking, Paul unwittingly reveals how perfectly submissive he was to the will of God. The ground, therefore, of his hope was the prayers of his friends.

2. The Source of His Hope

His hope's source is disclosed in the words, "I shall be granted unto you." There are only two words in the original, a verb and a pronoun, and they are very impressive. What Paul really says is, "I hope that through the prayers of you all, I shall be given to you all as a most gracious gift of God."

The Sovereign Will of God

Here, and habitually, Paul goes behind all events to the

sovereign and determining will of God. He could not, of course, be released from Rome except by Caesar's permission; but it is not Caesar who is in view here. Forces were operating for and against the Apostle. Had he regarded them alone, he might well have been distracted even to despair; but in the midst of all he was kept in perfect peace because his mind was stayed upon Jehovah. The activities alike of his friends at Colossae and his foes at Rome were looked at by the Apostle in the light of the will of God for him.

The Significance of the Word Which the Apostle Here Employs

The verb χαριζομαι is used in some striking connections: for example, "The things *freely given* to us of God" (1 Corinthians 2:12); "How shall He not also with Him *freely give* us all things? (Romans 8:32); "Ye . . . asked for a murderer *to be granted* unto you" (Acts 3:14); "No man can give me up unto them" (Acts 25:11).

The word has the force of "given as a favor from supreme authority," either for destruction (Acts 25:11), or for preservation (Acts 3:14). Now read the text again: "I hope that through the prayers of you all, I shall be *given* to you all *as a most gracious gift of God.*"

Paul would not think of his release from prison with reference to the pleasure that it would bring to him personally, but rather because of the profit that it would bring to the churches which he would visit. He wished *to-be-given* unto them for their service, comfort, and edification in Christ.

We have, therefore, in this word, not only the *source* of the Apostle's hope, which is God, but the *object* of it, which is the churches' enrichment.

The Content of the Pronoun Which Paul Uses

It is not, to "thee," Philemon, that he would be granted, but to "you," plural, "you all," already referred to at the beginning, but surely now including the man whom he is sending back with this very letter in his hand.

This is a delicate touch, and perhaps was not discerned, yet the influence of it must have been felt. As Paul thought of his possible release, and formed the purpose to visit his dear friend in the Lycus valley, not the least attractive element in the prospect was the hope that in that circle he would see Onesimus again, "no longer as a slave, but more than a slave, a brother beloved" (verse 16).

The idea of "you all" would not have been complete were that member of the circle to be absent.

So Paul hopes and, in his simple yet expressive language, tells what are the ground and source of that hope; the one, the prayers of the people, and the other, the gracious will of God.

Arising out of this hope is:

PAUL'S REQUEST FOR ACCOMMODATION

"But withal prepare me also a lodging; for I hope . . ."

We cannot fail, surely, to notice here:

1. THE APOSTLE'S MODESTY

What do you suppose it was that he wanted?

You have a dear friend in affluent circumstances, from whom through trouble you have been separated for years. You see your way out of your difficulties and, anxious to pay your friend a visit, you write and say: "I am hoping to be in the dear old town soon. Will you do me the kindness to locate me a room? I do not want anything elaborate, but would like the quarters to be as near you as possible, for I am yearning to see you all again."

So writing, what really would be in your mind, and would your friend be likely to reply to such a request? Your thought almost certainly would be Paul's, the wish to be Philemon's guest under his own roof, and your friend's reply would be Philemon's: "Overjoyed to think you are coming; my home and self are at your disposal."

Paul had been in a "lodging" for the last two years (Acts 28:23; ξενια as here; in only two occurrences in New Testament, a "hired house" as it is called in verse 30). That is all he is asking now, and perhaps in the request is the wish that it may be a place where, as in Rome, he might receive all who would wish to come to him for conversation and instruction concerning Jesus.

The "lodgings" Jerome says, "were for the Apostle rather than for Paul. He anticipated a large concourse of hearers. This would involve a situation convenient of access; large enough to hold a number of people; in a locality of good report, and undisturbed by a troublesome neighborhood." Certainly all these requirements would obtain in Philemon's own house, but Paul will not ask so much as that. Here again he would say, "Not as of necessity, but of free will" (verse 15).

This request brings to notice the whole matter of hospitality. To afford this is a signal service, and a great opportunity for those who are in a position to entertain. We cannot all help our fellow-Christians in the same way, but we can all help in some way.

What an unspeakable blessing a spare bedroom has been in some homes! How many of God's saints, tired ministers, homeless missionaries, and others have slept there, until the very walls are fragrant with their prayers and the home is full of benediction which their grateful hearts have prayed down.

Could not more of God's people exercise this grace of entertainment? It is the testimony of many that in doing so they have received more than they gave.

What more worthy record could one desire than that which Paul has given of a friend of his, "Gaius mine host, and of the whole Church." Who, do you suppose, was the more greatly blessed, the Apostle who was entertained, or the man who entertained him? And who, do you suppose, was the more blessed in that humble home at Bethany: Jesus, Who resorted thither in days of sorrow, or the three who received Him?

A whole world of Christian service lies open here to people who are in comfortable circumstances, and whose hearts are at leisure from themselves to soothe and sympathize. Paul's modesty was Philemon's opportunity, and I am confident he did not miss it.

2. THE APOSTLE'S MOTIVE

Lightfoot says, "There is a gentle compulsion in this mention of a personal visit to Colossae. The Apostle would thus be able to see for himself that Philemon had not disappointed his expectations." And Matthew Henry quaintly observes, passing from verse 21 and what precedes; "Paul comes to another thing, yet, as may seem, not without some eye to the matter which he had been upon, that might be furthered by his intimation that he hoped he should himself soon follow, and know the effect of his epistle, which Philemon would therefore be the more stirred up to see might be to his satisfaction."

Almost certainly these writers are correct in supposing that this final word of the Apostle's was intended also to supply Philemon with a final motive for receiving

Onesimus back again. The prospect of meeting would enhance the force of the Apostle's wish. If Philemon declined to grant his friend's request, or if he granted it only partially and grudgingly, how could he look Paul in the face when the liberated prisoner returned to Colossae?

Almost certainly Philemon, by this time, would not require the inspiration of this prospect to move him to what was a Christian duty and more, but it would tend, nevertheless, to increase his diligence and would encourage him to do more than Paul had said.

We also are furnished with such a motive. Our absent Lord has intimated that He is coming again, and there is no uncertainty attached to it. The prospect is sure and, so far from striking terror to our hearts, it should inspire us to lofty service and move us to generous deeds.

To have failed in our duty or to have only barely done it will not help us to anticipate our Lord's Return; but where hearts are gladly obedient and joyfully well-pleasing, the thought of His coming again will be an abiding inspiration.

If we give Him now a lodging in our hearts, He will one day give us mansions in the sky.

CONCLUSION

Salutations (23-24)

1. From One Fellow Prisoner

2. From Four Fellow Laborers

Benediction (25)

1. The Blessing

2. The Blessed

Verses 23-25

Epaphras, my fellow-prisoner in Christ Jesus, saluteth thee; and so do Mark, Aristarchus, Demas, Luke, my fellow-workers. The grace of our Lord Jesus Christ be with your spirit. Amen.

7

CONCLUSION (23-25)

This little letter ends as it began, with salutations. The Pauline salutations are not empty forms. Old Matthew Henry well says, "Christianity is no enemy to courtesy, but enjoins it." Salutations are universal and are expressions of goodwill and feeling among men, but the Apostolic salutations are more than this. May we never think it beneath our attention or dignity to exchange both by word and letter these friendly courtesies.

SALUTATIONS (23, 24)

You will observe that five names are mentioned, and they are divided into two categories, one being in the first — a fellow prisoner — and four in the second — fellow workers.

1. One Fellow Prisoner

"Epaphras, my fellow prisoner in Christ Jesus saluteth thee."

Epaphras was a Colossian (Colossians 4:12), and the spiritual guide of the Church there, and in all likelihood also of the assemblies in Laodicea and Hierapolis. No doubt he had heard Paul preach at Ephesus and, being blessed, had returned to his own town to found a church there.

In the Colossian salutations very much is said of him in few words.

> Epaphras, who is one of you, a servant of Christ Jesus, saluteth you, always agonizing for you in his prayers, that ye may stand perfect and fully assured in all the will of God. For I bear him witness, that he hath much labor for you, and for them in Laodicea, and for them in Hierapolis. (Colossians 4:12-13)

Errors both doctrinal and practical were threatening the Colossian Church, and Epaphras felt the need of taking counsel with his spiritual father and personal friend concerning them. For this purpose he had come to Rome; and it was the report which he had made to Paul which occasioned the letter to Colossae and furnished the opportunity, also, of sending back Onesimus with this little note.

The Apostle here refers to Epaphras as his "fellow prisoner." In the Colossian letter it is Aristarchus who is so spoken of. This variation has led to the conjecture that the Apostle's friends in Rome took it in turn to keep him company and were allowed to live with him, on condition of submitting to the same restrictions, military guardianship, and so on.

This suggestion is eminently probable and, if true, would throw an interesting light upon Paul's prison life, reflecting the devotion with which he was regarded by his many friends.

Whether in this or in any other way Epaphras became a prisoner, the captivity in this case, as in Paul's, was "in Christ Jesus."

Two important differences should be noted between this verse and verse one. In the first verse Paul speaks of himself as a "prisoner," δεσμιος ; in this verse he speaks of

Epaphras as a "prisoner," αἰχμάλωτος , with the prepositional prefix, συν. The former word means simply, "one bound," but the latter means "taken captive by the sword."

In its simple form the latter substantive occurs but once in the New Testament, in Luke 4:18, where Christ says that He was sent "to preach deliverance to the *captives.*" The verb occurs in but three passages which serve well to show its true force: Luke 21:24 — *"They . . . shall be led captive* into all nations"; Romans 7:23 — "I see a different law in my members, warring against the law of my mind, and *bringing me into captivity* under the law of sin"; 2 Corinthians 10:5 — *"Bringing* every thought *into captivity* to the obedience of Christ." In the compound form it occurs only in Romans 16:7, Colossians 4:10, and here; and the verb does not occur at all.

Paul uses both words of himself. In verse 1, *he is bound,* and in verse 23 he considers himself *a captive of war;* yet, in neither instance is he the captive of Nero or of Rome.

Epaphras is honored to be associated with him in this captivity, for, in both cases, it is on account of their faith in and loyalty to Jesus Christ.

The other difference between these verses is that, in one, Paul is a prisoner "of Christ Jesus," but in this verse, he and Epaphras are captives "in Christ Jesus." In the first expression reference is made to *the author* of his captivity, but, in the second, to *the sphere* of it.

How sublimely Paul ignores all secondary agencies and all material surroundings. It is Christ who has made him a prisoner, not Nero; and it is in Christ that he is held as a war captive, not in the Roman prison, nor as a war trophy of Rome.

What unspeakable peace to the soul such a view of our afflictions would bring, and what motive and power for endurance!

Epaphras then, is Paul's "fellow-prisoner." It would be difficult to say which of them derived the greater benefit from such an association: whether Epaphras, by receiving Paul's counsel, or Paul, by receiving Epaphras' comfort. Certain it is that each would be greatly enriched and would spend together prolonged and blessed seasons of prayer, for in this they both were giants (Colossians 4:12).

There is very much of truth in the saying that "joys shared are doubled; sorrows shared are halved." The double experience resulted from this companionship in the Roman prison, and Paul is not slow to acknowledge it.

God sometimes lightens the sufferings of His servants by the communion of saints, the sweet fellowship they have one with another in their bonds. Never more enjoyment of God have they found than when suffering together for God. So Paul and Silas, when they had their feet fast in the stocks, had their tongues set at liberty, and their hearts tuned for the praises of God.

Paul's mention of the Colossian in this relation and connection was designed, like all that has gone before, to help Philemon to the generous fulfilment of his request on the behalf of Onesimus.

1. Four Fellow Laborers

"Mark, Aristarchus, Demas, Luke, my fellow laborers."

The first two of these are Jews and the other two are Gentiles. They are all mentioned in the Colossian letter, though not in this order or with this brevity.

To each of these men a very real though not an equal interest attaches, and the mention of their names should be to us encouragement or warning. What is there more interesting than people! Let us briefly recall what is known of these four.

Mark. This young man was the son of Mary, who was so hospitable to the saints at Jerusalem and whose house was the place of meeting for prayer and the worship of God (Acts 12:12). He was also the cousin of Barnabas who accompanied Paul on his first missionary journey (Colossians 4:10).

He appears to have been the convert of Peter (1 Peter 5:13), whose influence dominated his outlook and gave shape and color to the Gospel which he wrote, the earliest of the four.

When Paul and Barnabas set out on their first journey, Mark accompanied them as far as to Perga in Pamphylia and then returned home. This led later to a difference between Paul and Barnabas which, so far as we know, was never made good, though a reconciliation took place between Paul and Mark as this passage and 2 Timothy 4:11 show. Tradition says Mark became the bishop of Alexandria.

These particulars summarize what we know of John Mark, who at this time was evidently residing in Rome (Colossians 4:10; Philemon 24) and was contemplating a visit to proconsular Asia. His name in our letter to Philemon conveys this message of hope among others: that differences between friends can be made good and regrettable estrangements can and should end in enduring reconciliation.

Aristarchus. Little is said of this brother in the New Testament, but from the glimpse or two we get of him, we learn that he was devoted to Paul and the Gospel, and suffered for both.

He is first mentioned as having been seized, together with Gaius, during the great riot at Ephesus and rushed into the theatre, where, certainly, his life was in danger (Acts 19:29).

In the next reference he is seen accompanying Paul from Troas on his last journey to Jerusalem (Acts 20:4) and thereafter on his passage to Rome (27:2).

At the time that Paul wrote the Colossian letter and this note to Philemon, Aristarchus was with him, both a fellow prisoner (Colossians 4:10) and fellow worker.

It has been thought that, as Aristarchus in Colossians and Epaphras in Philemon are Paul's fellow prisoners, these participated in the Apostle's bonds alternately and that therefore their imprisonment was voluntary.

What is sure is that Aristarchus was a devoted friend, and by sharing in Paul's sufferings and service brought him both comfort and help.

It is not likely that much will be said about any of us after we are dead, but it is most important that what is said be to our credit and the glory of God.

With his two Jewish friends Paul now associates two Gentiles.

Demas. Demas! What does that name suggest to you? We read of this man only three times: in Colossians 4:14, in our text, and in 2 Timothy 4:10-11; and in each instance he is mentioned with Luke. In Colossians he is just mentioned as associated with the salutation. In our text, beyond that, he is spoken of as Paul's fellow worker. And in the final passage Paul says to Timothy, "Give diligence to come shortly unto me; for Demas forsook me, having loved this present world, and went to Thessalonica."

Between the writing of the first two of these Letters and

the third, some four years elapsed, and in that time Demas ceased to be a fellow worker and became a deserter.

We naturally ask, why? and how? The only help we have towards an answer to these questions is in the phrase "having loved this present world." But what does that mean? Was it that he "followed the way of Balaam the son of Bosor, who loved the hire of wrong-doing" (2 Peter 2:15)? Did he become a lucre-cankered soul? Or, is it that, as others in his time, he apostatized from the Christian faith? Or, did he, when he saw the clouds gathering in Paul's sky and heard the ominous rumbling of opposition, prove a coward and play for safety?

We do not know. But this we know: that he fell all the distance that he had risen, and the man had risen high who had become a fellow worker with the Apostle Paul.

Demas proved disloyal to friendship, untrue to himself, and faithless to God. In the light of the last reference to him, the mention of his name with the others in our text brings a shadow across an otherwise sunny page.

Let us all beware of disloyalty to the highest and best we have ever known.

But there is yet another name, the most outstanding of the group.

Luke. What Sir Thomas Browne was to Bishop Joseph Hall, that Luke was to Paul.

Of the great men of the New Testament, Luke is one of the greatest. This estimate will not seem exaggerated when we think, on the one hand, of what he did for and meant to the greatest of the apostles, and, on the other hand, of his contributions to the literature of the New Testament. What should we do without the third Gospel and the book of Acts?

There are few outstanding New Testament characters of whom we know so little, and of whom we would fain know so much, as St. Luke.

Was Luke the man whom Paul saw in his vision, beckoning him to come over to Macedonia? So Sir William Ramsay thinks. At any rate, we know that he was the Apostle's constant companion and best friend, of whom he wrote at the last, "only Luke is with me."

A man of culture, of medical knowledge and skill, an author, a traveller, and a man of cheery temperament as his Gospel and the Acts show; a man true as steel, and withal of sterling Christian character, he was valuable beyond all price to the great Apostle as he prosecuted his immense task.

Luke attended to his friend's health, kept his memoranda, guided him in his courses, cheered him in sorrow, encouraged him in his labors, and had fellowship with him in prayers.

And, at the last, when many of his friends could not be with him, and others had forsaken him, Luke remained true and was at Paul's side, we must suppose, to the last. Well may the Apostle speak of him as "the beloved physician," and "my fellow worker." Demas might have learned his lesson better, yoked as he was with such a man as Luke.

These then are the men whom Paul here associates with himself in the salutation he sends to Philemon and his household: Epaphras, Mark, Aristarchus, Demas, and Luke.

You will observe that Paul calls these his fellow workers, or fellow laborers. He had so spoken of Philemon, in verse 1.

This point is an important one, for in directions it is thought that if one wants a soft job he should go into the Christian ministry. But our Lord said, "Pray ye therefore the Lord of the harvest, that He send forth *laborers* [not loiterers] into His harvest" (Matthew 9:38). And Paul exhorts the Thessalonians "to know those that *labor* among them."

But all who are engaged in Christian service are fellow laborers. Both parts of the word are emphatic. We are fellow *laborers* if we have at all apprehended the importance and dimensions of the task to which we have been appointed; and we are *fellow* laborers if we understand at all the spirit of Christian service, a service which we should never enter for personal or sectarian ends. If Christianity is to win its way in the world, it will only be by the hearty, diligent, and loyal cooperation of all who are in this fellowship of faith.

When we understand this aright, we shall better appreciate the truth of 1 Corinthians 12 — the diversity of gifts in the unity of the body.

Epaphras, Mark, Aristarchus, Demas, Luke. These are only a few of Paul's very many friends, some of whose names appear in the New Testament. We naturally think of Barnabas, Silas, Timothy, Apollos, Titus, Epaphroditus, and Onesiphorus, as well as Philemon and Onesimus, and many another.

Paul had a wonderful genius for friendship, and an examination of the above names will serve to show how diverse were the men whom he attracted to himself; men learned and unlearned, well-to-do and poor, Jews and Gentiles all alike found in him one whom they could trust and love, and just because he loved and trusted them all.

Every kindness they showed him he gratefully acknowledged, and every departure from love and loyalty he greatly mourned.

If Paul, by recording the names of the faithful, has immortalized them in the hearts of all who love loyalty, by mentioning the names of *others,* such as Demas,

Hymenaeus, and Demetrius, he has made them for all time examples to be avoided. Of these he would say,

Blot out his name, then record one lost soul more, One task more declined, one more footpath untrod, One more devil's-triumph and sorrow for angels, One wrong more to man, one more insult to God!

It is something to fear to be judged a recreant by people of high principle and wide sympathies, as it is something to receive their admiration and gratitude.

True friendships, friendships which stand the test of storm and time are comparatively few, but such are very precious. Yet, perhaps, it is true and well to say that we might all be more friendly, and so enrich ourselves in the effort, to bless others.

If we cannot all be *fellow prisoners,* we can at any rate be *fellow soldiers* (verse 2), and *fellow workers* (verses 1, 23).

BENEDICTION (25)

"The grace of our Lord Jesus Christ be with your spirit. Amen."

The letter began with a benediction (verse 3), and there we studied the blessings and blessers. To these the Apostle again returns.

1. THE BLESSING.

"The grace of our Lord Jesus Christ."

This simple phrase is very profound, telling as it does what are the *nature* and *source* of the blessing sought.

The Nature of the Blessing — "Grace."

We have already seen that grace stands for the whole sum of the unmerited blessings which come to men through Jesus Christ. It is the unconditional, undeserved, spontaneous, eternal, stooping, pardoning love of God.

If we have this "grace," we have in some sense every blessing, and for this reason Paul begins this and others of his letters on this great note.

The Source of the Blessing "The Lord Jesus Christ."

On this title the letter begins and ends (verse 3). At the beginning "grace and peace" have a double source; they are "from God our Father and the Lord Jesus Christ"; but here, "grace" — peace not being mentioned — is traced to the Son only.

The reason for this is that Christ is the focus of the grace of God. As the rays of the sun may be gathered, focussed, and distributed through a powerful lens, so the fulness of God is concentrated in and distributed from and by the Lord Jesus Christ. The fact that Christ is associated with God the Father, as He is in verse 3, and is spoken of in the same connection alone in this verse is undesigned witness to the Apostle's belief in His full and proper Deity; and in the title given Him there is a fulness reached which is comprehensive: "The Lord" and "Jesus" meeting in "The Christ."

When that One is the source of blessing, we may be quite sure of the sufficiency and regularity of the supply.

2. The Blessed

"Grace be with your spirit."

The pronoun employed leads us to think of

The Fellowship of the Blessed.

The pronoun "your" does not refer only to Philemon, but to his family and the Church in his house (verses 1-2). It is plural and therefore comprehensive.

As blessing never comes alone, so it never comes only to one. Wherever there is one blessing there is a second; and whenever one person is blessed, inevitably so are others. Blessing is social and cannot exist alone. So Paul prays this prayer on behalf of that Colossian company and all Christians.

The Sphere in Which We are Blessed — "Your Spirit."

"Grace in the spirit," says Jerome, "spiritualizes the whole man." "Grace has man's spirit for the field of its highest operation. Thither it can enter, and there it can abide, in union more close and communion more real and blessed than aught else can attain. The spirit which has the grace of Christ with it can never be utterly solitary or desolate."

At the end of all Paul writes "Amen," a word expressive of desire and confidence. By it he means, not only "may it be so," but "surely it shall be so."

It! What is under cover of that?

All that this precious letter has made our glad possession. Maclaren summarizes its teaching in an impressive way when he says, "In this letter, the central springs of Christian service are touched, and the motives used to sway Philemon are the echo of the motives which Christ uses to sway men."

The keynote of all is love. Love beseeches when it might command. To love we owe our ownselves beside.

Love will do nothing without the glad consent of Him to whom it speaks and cares for no service which is of necessity. Its finest wine is not made from juice which is pressed out of grapes, but that which flows from them for very ripeness.

Love identifies itself with those who need its help, and treats with kindness to them as done to itself. Love finds joy and heart-solace in willing, though it be imperfect service. Love expects more than it asks. Love hopes for reunion, and by the hope makes its wish more mighty. These are the points of Paul's pleading with Philemon. Are they not the elements of Christ's pleading with His friends? To all this Paul adds, "Amen"; and to it all we would say, "Amen." Here we see Christianity at work, here we see the highest principles brought to bear upon the smallest details of everyday life, and here, also, we see how all-conquering is the love of God when it is shed abroad in our hearts by the Holy Spirit.

PRACTICAL APPLICATION

The Manifold Values of This Epistle

1. Personal Value

2. Ethical Value

3. Providential Value

4. Practical Value

5. Evangelical Value

6. Social Value

7. Spiritual Value

8

PRACTICAL APPLICATION

The Manifold Values of This Epistle

Renan has spoken of this little letter as a *note,* and that is really what it is.

It is quite unique in the Pauline group of writings, and consequently a special interest attaches to it. Short as the letter is, it has manifold values which make it very precious, values at once personal, ethical, providential, practical, evangelical, social, and spiritual.

Its Personal Value consists in the light which it throws upon the character of Paul.

Its Ethical Value consists in its balanced sensitiveness to what is right.

Its Providential Value consists in its underlying suggestion that God is behind and above all events.

Its Practical Value consists in its application of the highest principles to the commonest affairs.

Its Evangelical Value consists in the encouragement it supplies to seek and to redeem the lowest.

Its Social Value consists in its presentation of the relation of Christianity to slavery and all unchristian institutions.

Its Spiritual Value consists in the analogy between it and the Gospel story.

From this it will be abundantly evident that this little note has a value altogether out of proportion to its size. The primitive Church regarded it as scarcely worthy of a place in the Canon of Sacred Writings, and many concluded, on account of the absence of any approach to doctrinal teaching in it, that it was not from the hand of Paul at all. But, happily, this kind of criticism did not prevail against the common acceptance of its authenticity.

At this late date only the most wanton skepticism will call into question its genuineness. It is hard to conceive how anyone can read it without feeling that we have in it a picture of the Apostle of the Gentiles, which we could ill afford to lose, but which no hand except his own would have ventured to paint. Let us therefore look briefly at the several values of this little note.

1. Its Personal Value

Its personal value consists in the light which it throws upon the character of Paul.

Paul's Private Correspondence

If Hebrews be excluded, we have from this Apostle thirteen letters. Nine of these are written to seven churches; three are written to two individuals, giving authoritative direction concerning belief and order in the assemblies, and one only is purely personal and strictly private.

During the course of his ministry, Paul must have written hundreds of letters, both official and personal, but these thirteen only have been preserved, and of the private correspondence, only this little Note to Philemon.

Accordingly, the Apostle is here seen in a new light, and so impressive is the view that we are left longing that more of this kind of correspondence might have been preserved.

Letter-writing is a great art, and when it is made the vehicle of spiritual fellowship, the product is a priceless treasure. Classic illustrations of this we have in the letters of Rutherford, Newton and McCheyne.

In the Rutherford Collection there is a letter for every day of the year, and if you wish a course of spiritual instruction, you could scarcely do better than read one a day, unless, indeed, you do the same with John Newton's *Cardiphonia.*

Let us from this priceless gem of Paul's private correspondence, this "pure pearl of a letter," as Maclaren calls it, learn how to conduct our own letter writing.

One feature of character which this Note strongly shows us is:

Paul's Tender Solicitude

Mark the way in which he speaks of his new slave-convert, Onesimus. This wild youth is his "child"; Paul has "begotten" him; Onesimus is "profitable" to him; he is his "very heart"; he is a "brother beloved," and he is, Paul says, "as myself."

Paul has been thought to be severe and forbidding, a man austere and unemotional; but such is far from being the case. He had a womanly-like tenderness, and, as he told the Thessalonians, he was among them "gentle, even as a nurse cherisheth her children."

He could, of course, be stern when occasion required it, and his quality in his character comes out in his Letters to Corinth and Galatia.

Gentleness that is not capable of being severe is a weakness; and so is severity that cannot be gentle. In a truly great character these will combine and be displayed under the direction of a wise discrimination.

But, perhaps, what is most distinctive of the little Note, in the personal aspect of it, is

Paul's Consummate Tact

This fact, as we have seen in the exposition of the Letter, is exhibited at every turn, in almost every sentence, and in his choice of words.

It is displayed, also, in what he does not say. Mark the way in which he introduces himself. He is not the Apostle, but a "prisoner," and "aged."

Mark also his approach to the matter in hand. He recognizes and commends the good that stands to Philemon's credit, and exhorts him to continue in it. And further, observe the place and way in which he mentions Onesimus. The name does not occur until verse 10, and then at the end of it. "I beseech thee for my child, whom I have begotten in my bonds — Onesimus."

Then there is his resolve to entreat where he might have enjoined. Paul might have urged the reinstatement of Onesimus as a Christian duty, but he takes other ground.

And see how he makes himself personally responsible for the discharge of the debt. Not for a moment is the moral tone lowered. Wrong had been done, and it must be righted.

In these and many other ways the consummate tact of the Apostle is displayed. One writer has well said, "We seem to know St. Paul better, even as an Apostle, because we are allowed to see him when he chooses not to be an Apostle, but a 'partner.'" But, even beyond this, we may fairly draw from this Epistle a priceless lesson as to the place which true courtesy and delicacy occupy in Christian character. We feel, as we read, how little it accords with the idea that Christian men and Christian ministers "have nothing to do with being gentlemen."

We understand how true courtesy, as distinct from artificial and technical culture of manners, is the natural outgrowth of the lowliness of mind in which "each esteems other better than himself" (Philippians 2:3).

The cultivation by us of this quality would not only make all our work so much easier of accomplishment but would commend so much more to the world the Gospel which we are called to adorn.

2. Its Ethical Value

Its ethical value consists in its balanced sensitiveness to what is right.

The Sinfulness of Onesimus' Act

Onesimus is made to feel the sinfulness of his act. Though he does not unnecessarily dwell upon it or employ terms concerning it which were needlessly harsh, yet, what he does say can leave no one in any doubt as to his view.

He declares that this man had been altogether false to his name; called "profitable," he had been "unprofitable," a good-for-nothing, a bad-for-everything.

He says plainly that Onesimus had wronged Philemon, and he implies by the use of the word *owe* that he was a thief.

The story was a dark one, the record was very bad; and we need not doubt that Paul had rubbed this well into the mind, heart, and conscience of the slave himself at the time he was pointing him to the way of salvation.

The Need for Reparation

Onesimus is further given to understand that reparation must be made. The new life does not cancel the old debts. The Gospel of Jesus Christ requires that wrongs be righted. Immediately upon the return of a wrongdoer to the path of right, the conscience dictates the adjustment of what has been wrong, dictates that amends be made, as far as that be possible, for the injustices of the past.

So Zacchaeus said, "Behold, Lord, the half of my goods I give to the poor; and if I have wrongfully exacted aught from any man, I restore him four-fold" (Luke 19:2).

That Paul brought this home to Onesimus is beyond question. But this penniless runaway had no means of making reparation. What, then, was to be done? Paul did not say to him, "Well, as you have nothing, you cannot pay." Paul represented it as so essential that the sin should cost, that he himself undertook to pay the debt, probably by making tents in his prison house; and that, more than anything else, would make Onesimus feel how grievous was his offence and how imperious were the claims of right and justice.

The Over-riding of Personal Desires

The slave is sent back to his master though Paul would have liked to keep him. Paul would not allow affectionate desires and personal convenience to interfere with social obligations.

The slave was Philemon's, and if Paul had kept him at Rome, he would be doing his Colossian friend an injustice or else taking a mean advantage of him. Paul would do neither. The boy must go back, though in doing so he was exposing himself to the punishment which his wrongdoing merited, according to the standard of judgment of that time.

Surely no one was ever more sensitive to what is fit and right than was Paul. His conscience was essentially ethical. To him Christianity was intensely practical. I wonder if this can be said of us!

3. Its Providential Value

Its providential value consists in its underlying suggestion that God is around, behind, and above all events.

Paul says, "For perhaps he was therefore parted from thee for a season that thou shouldest have him for ever" (15). This utterance is pregnant with suggestion, the nature and force of which one or two observations will show.

Responsibility for Free Acts

Onesimus acted in the freedom of his depraved will. What he did, he did voluntarily and wickedly and, in this instance, without provocation. He, therefore, must take entire responsibility for his conduct and could have had no ground of complaint had the full consequences of it come upon him.

Had he suffered the penalty which the times imposed upon such conduct, in all likelihood he would have been crucified.

That that sinful act of his, the final expression of a sinful career, was turned to good account, in no wise mitigates his offense, and for any beneficent result that followed, he could take no credit. We may never do evil that good may come; but, in this instance, there was no idea or intention that good would come out of his reckless conduct.

The Role of Providence

Behind this slave's will was the divine wisdom controlling the results. The whole truth of Providence is more or less wrapped in mystery, but the facts bear witness to it through all the ages of history. Out of the eater God has ever been bringing forth meat, and out of the strong, sweetness.

He makes the wrath of men to praise Him; all things serve Him. His purposes are fulfilled, if not by means of us, then, in spite of us. God is sovereign in His universe notwithstanding human and angelic free-will. He is the mighty Worker who can transmute even sin and make the finished wickedness of men to be their first step to glory.

Let it be said again, with all the emphasis possible, that this in no degree diminishes the sinfulness of sin, and on Divine Providence men must never presume.

Yet, in the infinite mercy of God, not only others, but the sinner himself is often blessed by the exercise of such providence, as witness the case before us.

God can overrule all, just because He rules over all. This truth is of far-reaching application, and must convey immense comfort to the people of God, especially in our own time.

Providence's Independence from Sin

Paul safeguards this fact from the appearance of making the slave's sin a necessity for his salvation. He says, "perhaps," which we certainly may take to mean that God could have reached and rescued Onesimus in some other way.

If any man's salvation depended upon his indulging in some sin or other, then, in order to accomplish that end, he would be justified in sinning.

Paul will not allow himself to be chargeable with such an idea, and so, though in the case before him salvation actually eventuated, he will not say emphatically that Onesimus was allowed thus to sin in order to be saved. He prefers to be indefinite on that point, lest a wholly false inference be drawn, or an unholy use be made of the circumstance. "Perhaps." Where Paul left it, we may safely leave it.

4. ITS PRACTICAL VALUE

Its practical value consists in its application of the highest principles to the commonest affairs of life.

The Practical Nature of Christian Principles

Christian principles are essentially practical in character. The sphere of their activity is our common life. No further evidence of this is needed than that which these prison Letters supply. The first half of the Letter to Ephesus is profoundly doctrinal, and the latter half is intensely practical. Nowhere in his writings does the Apostle take higher flights into the realms of truth than in the twin Epistles to Ephesus and Colossae; and yet nowhere is there a stronger insistence upon practical Christianity, upon the working out of the Christian revelation in all the relations and circumstances of life.

Paul's doctrine is that we are to believe rightly in order to walk worthily. The highest truths are designed for practical ends.

Christianity's Uniqueness

Because of its practical nature, Christianity differs from all the religions of the world. While some of these enshrine noble ethical ideals, none of them impart power for holy living. The best of them, at their best, only point to a far off and unattainable good; they are wholly lacking in spiritual dynamic. They offer theories for acceptance and leave the soul sick unto despair.

Not so Christianity. It lies alongside the life of us all, and not only points to the right road, but places our feet therein, and keeps us walking therein. It tells us what is right, and enables us to do it. Its highest principles are capable of lowliest applications. Its richest flowers bloom in common soil. Its priceless treasures are poured at the feet of us all.

The Application of Christian Principles

The way in which these principles are applied should always be characterized by the spirit of their author.

No better example of this can be furnished than the little Note before us. It has been well said that here, "Paul speaks with that peculiar grace of humility and courtesy which has, under the reign of Christianity, developed the spirit of chivalry and what is called the character of a gentleman — certainly very little known in the old Greek and Roman civilizations. Yet in its graceful flexibility and vivacity it stands contrasted with the more impassive oriental stateliness."

The younger Pliny wrote a letter to a friend on an occasion similar to this. It has often been brought into comparison with Paul's Note; and the least that can be said is that the Apostle's letter does not suffer from the comparison. Pliny wrote:

Your freedman, with whom you had told me you were vexed, came to me and throwing himself down before me clung to my feet, as if they had been yours. He was profuse in his tears and his entreaties; he was profuse also in his silence. In short, he convinced me of his penitence. I believe that he is indeed a reformed character, because he feels that he has done wrong. You are angry, I know; and you have reason to be angry, this also I know; but mercy wins the highest praise just when there is the most righteous cause for anger. You loved the man and, I hope, will continue to love him; meanwhile, it is enough that you should allow yourself to yield to his prayers. You may be angry again, if he deserves it; and in this you will be the more readily pardoned if you yield now. Concede something to his youth, something to his tears, something to your own indulgent disposition. Do not torture him, lest you torture yourself at the same time. For it is torture to you, when one of your gentle temper is angry. I am afraid lest I should appear not to ask but to compel, if I should add my prayers to his. Yet I will add them the more fully and unreservedly, because I scolded the man himself with sharpness and severity; for I threatened him straitly that I would never ask you again. This I said to him, for it was necessary to alarm him; but I do not use the same language to you. For perchance I shall ask again, and shall be successful again; only let my request be such, as it becomes me to prefer and you to grant. Farewell.

Of these two letters Lightfoot says:

The younger Pliny is the noblest type of a true Roman gentleman, and this touching letter needs no words of praise. Yet, if purity of diction be excepted, there will hardly be any difference of opinion in awarding the palm to the Christian Apostle. As an expression of simple dignity, of refined courtesy, of large sympathy, and of warm personal affection, the Epistle to Philemon stands unrivalled. And its pre-eminence is the more remarkable because in style it is exceptionally loose. It owes nothing to the graces of rhetoric; its effect is due solely to the spirit of the writer.

Truly the Apostle's letter is a practical commentary on his own injunction in the Epistle to the Colossians (4:6), "Let your speech be always with grace seasoned with salt."

5. ITS EVANGELICAL VALUE

Its evangelical value consists in the encouragement it supplies to seek and redeem the lowest.

The Gospel's Universal Power

The incident related in this letter shows that no one is beyond reclamation.

We cannot take a too serious view of the depravity of human nature, but we may, and often do, gravely underestimate the power of God. No one will deny that sin abounds; but all are tempted, at times, to question whether grace can much more abound.

Let a Christian worker once come to regard anyone as beyond reclamation and his usefulness in that direction is at an end.

This is a day in which we are exhorted to have faith in human nature. The Bible nowhere puts such a strain upon our faith, but it does exhort us to believe that, Christ is able to save to the uttermost all who come to God by Him; and the truth of this claim has been demonstrated millions of times.

Remember Baedeker among the Russian convicts; Jerry McAuley, "Down in Water Street"; Paton, among the cannibals of the New Hebrides; the Salvation Army in the slums of the world — and then say if there are any who are beyond reclaim.

Charles Darwin pronounced the Patagonians the missing link between man and monkey and thought that not even the lever of Christian missions could uplift them. They had low foreheads, but lower minds and morals, wretched hovels, and scant clothing. At times they were like brute beasts; at others, treacherous robbers.

But Allen Gardiner went among them with the Gospel, and the mighty miracle was wrought. So astonished was Darwin at the results that he became a regular subscriber of the South American Missionary Society.

Yes, the Gospel that could save Onesimus can save anyone, and with this little letter to Philemon, in heart, and head, and hand, let the evangelist go to the ends of the earth.

The power to reclaim is not ours, but it is that Spirit's at whose bidding we go, and Who, let us ever remember, has been at work in human hearts before we arrive. We are called, not only to sow, but to reap.

Christ saw Nathanael before the latter saw Christ; and the Spirit of God had begun operations in Onesimus before the slave and Paul met. Let us ever go forward presuming upon a work already commenced.

The Gospel's Elevating Power

We see here the power of the Gospel to bring out the hidden qualities of a down-trodden class. There are heroisms slumbering in more breasts than we think; there are shrivelled powers in most men that but await the kisses of the Son to bring them to full realization. No class of the community in Paul's day was so entirely degraded and so utterly hopeless as were the slaves. Their masters could think nothing too bad of them, and they lived down to that reputation.

Yet, though all unsuspected, deep down in their hearts, feelings lay buried which grace could restore; there was tenderness which only awaited someone to appeal to it, loyalty which required only to be trusted. Undreamed of possibilities lay buried and crushed in the heart of slavedom for want of the Gospel message and an opportunity to respond to it.

That this was so the case of Onesimus proves.

From what Paul says of him in this Letter, he was a youth capable of winning strong affection; for Paul speaks of him as his "very heart" (verse 12). He also had the ability to be very useful, to be really true to his name (verse 11); and Paul would have kept him so that Onesimus might have served him in many practical ways (verse 13), but he sent him back to render such service to his master (verse 16). There were, evidently, not a few admirable qualities in this youth so typical of the worst kind of slave, and the grace of God discovered them and released them for the service of mankind.

Lightfoot says:

> The great capacity for good which appears in the typical slave of Greek and Roman fiction, notwithstanding all the fraud and profligacy overlying it, was evoked and developed here by the inspiration of a new faith and the incentive of a new hope. The genial, affectionate, winning disposition, purified and elevated by a higher knowledge, had found its proper scope.

Let us, then, in our service for God, look for things in people that, under the fructifying influence of grace, would make them a power and a blessing to society.

Sympathetic Evangelists

These facts should lead us into sympathetic contact with those whom we would win. We are frequently fatally wrong in our approach to sinners, and we would be well advised to study how Paul approached them and, better still, how his and our Master approached them.

While Paul would not fail to talk to Onesimus about his sin, I am sure that was not the burden of his conversation but rather the grace and power and beauty of the Savior.

Paul would not first point out to this slave his moral obligation and then bid him take Christ to help him fulfil it. Rather would he first furnish him with spiritual motive and dynamic and then show him all his duty. Then, let this great master be our teacher, and we shall more often succeed.

6. Its Social Value

Its social value consists in its disclosure of the relation of Christianity to slavery and all unchristian institutions.

Throughout the whole Bible story we are face to face with the slave. In the Old Testament, slavery was recognized, though not established, by the Mosaic Law, and the hard lot of slaves was, under the Hebrew system, considerably mitigated.

This should occasion no surprise when we remember the essentially imperfect preparatory character of the Jewish covenant. The Old Testament is not the final Word of God and, therefore, cannot be appealed to as a complete and final expression of the mind of God, on slavery or any other subject.

We must remember the relativity of Biblical utterances and recognize that some laws were adapted to given regrettable circumstances, to be replaced by better when the ethical temper of society improved. The recognition of this fact would, on the one hand, have prevented anyone appealing to the Old Testament in justification of slavery; and, on the other hand, it would have saved the opponents of slavery from intellectual embarrassment.

In the New Testament, also, we are face to face with slavery, though there it nowhere receives endorsement. The slaves were the lowest and most unhappy class of Graeco-Roman Society; they were just live-chattels.

The present working or wage-earning class was unknown to ancient civilization; slaves were regarded as the property of their masters. But with the advent of Christ new conceptions of human duties and relationships entered the world, and the poor had the Gospel preached to them.

The letter before us leads us to observe:

Christianity's Non-political Nature

Christianity is not a political movement and, therefore, does not antagonize forms of government.

Forms of government are for the nations, but Christianity is for the world. It indeed acts upon individuals which compose the nations, and so in course of time transforms from within the institutions of the country.

But it does not attack them from without; and, therefore, it is compatible with any form of government.

Christianity's Just Nature

Christianity is, in principle, opposed to every form of injustice; and wherever it is operative, it establishes social order on the foundation of righteousness.

Social order is not socialism. Christianity does not merely recognize social order, but defines and establishes it both in the home, and in the state:

In the home — Ephesians 5:22 — 6:9; Colossians

3:18 — 4:1; I Peter 2:18 — 3:7.

In the state — Romans 13; I Timothy 2:1-2; I Peter 2:17.

But while establishing such an order, Christianity introduces a new doctrine, applicable only to the redeemed, that is, that in Christ all distinctions are done away:

I Corinthians 7:21-22; Galatians 3:26-28; Colossians 3:10-11.

Let it, however, be remembered that the fact of social order and the truth of differences obliterated do not conflict. Both should be recognized by all Christians and harmonized in a life that is designed and controlled by the Spirit of God. Christian masters and servants, mistresses and maids, employers and employees should recognize their respective obligations in the fear and grace of God. Only so can the Christian ideal be realized.

The story before us proves the truth of Bishop Wordsworth's saying, "The Gospel by Christianizing the master has enfranchised the slave."

One other point must be observed, namely,

Christianity's Transformative Method

Christianity is not revolutionary but transformative in its method.

The object of revolutionary movements is to destroy all forms of government, to overturn all institutions, to annihilate all class distinctions, and to sweep away all traditions; and they leave to future generations the thankless task of reconstructing society out of the ruins left by their relentless destructive policy.

There is no more tragic proof and illustration of this than Russia at the present time. Communism is a handmaid to all such movements. That economic system or theory upholds the absorption of all rights in a common interest, an equitable division of labor, and the formation of a common fund for the supply of all the wants of the community.

With this doctrine of a community of property or the negation of individual rights in property, Christianity has nothing to do. It is the poles asunder from Marxianism. Neither is it the ally of either captial or labor.

Christianity meddles directly with no political or social arrangements, but lays down principles which profoundly affect these, and leaves them to soak into the general mind.

Its method is not one of revolution but of transformation. Had an attack been made in Paul's day on the system of slavery, it would have precipitated a social convulsion; the whole force of imperial Rome would have arisen against Christianity; and a frightful revolution would have resulted from a rising of the slaves against their masters.

But the Christian method was otherwise. Christians had to show at the very outset that Christianity was not inconsistent with good citizenship, and that the reforms which it hoped to promote in social life would not be imposed violently from without, but that they would be the outcome of the development of a national conscience in which the seed of the Gospel was to grow and fructify secretly but surely.

Instead of attacking special abuses, Christianity lays down universal principles which shall undermine the evil.

It is not concerned with the fruits, but with the roots of things. Paul has no word of reproach for the masters on the injustice of their position; he breathes no hint to the slaves of a social grievance needing redress.

Suppose he had done so and the slave population, which was four times as numerous as the citizen population, had been emancipated — what then? Were the slaves capable of governing themselves or of being governed on equitable terms with freemen?

Paul saw a long way ahead, and left the Cross to do its work in its own time and way.

Centuries were to pass before the implications of the Gospel with reference to this institution would be widely felt and acted upon. But that time came; and what Paul commenced, Wilberforce, to a large extent, completed.

All this marks off Christianity, not only as unique, but as the only hope for anyone. If social evils are ever to be adjusted, Christianity must be the motive and the power.

7. Its Spiritual Value

Its spiritual value consists in the analogy which the circumstances bear to the Gospel story.

This analogy has not been better put than in the words of Luther:

> This Epistle showeth a right noble lovely example of Christian love. Here we see how St. Paul layeth himself out for the poor Onesimus, and with all his means pleadeth his cause with his master; and so setteth himself, as if he were Onesimus, and had himself done wrong to Philemon.
>
> Yet all this doeth he not with power or force, as if he had right thereto; but he strippeth himself of his right and thus enforced Philemon to forego his right also.
>
> Even as Christ did for us with God the Father, thus also doth St. Paul for Onesimus with Philemon; for Christ also stripped Himself of His right, and by love and humility enforced the Father to lay aside His wrath and power, and to take us to His grace for the sake of Christ, who lovingly pleadeth our cause, and

with all His heart layeth Himself out for us.
For we are all His Onesimi to my thinking.

With that we may close, deeply thankful for this precious little Letter, and eternally grateful for our own experience of the grace of God which it reflects.

"Grace to you and peace from God our Father and the Lord Jesus Christ. The grace of our Lord Jesus Christ be with your spirit. Amen."